KU-760-249

Lessons for EMU from the History of Monetary Unions

Michael D. Bordo
Rutgers University, New Jersey

and

Lars Jonung
Stockholm School of Economics

With an Introduction by Robert A. Mundell

and Commentaries by

Sir Samuel Brittan

Lord Currie of Marylebone

Walter Eltis

David Laidler

Anna J. Schwartz

Sir Alan Walters

Published by The Institute of Economic Affairs 2000

First published in May 2000 by
The Institute of Economic Affairs
2 Lord North Street
Westminster
London SW1P 3LB

IEA Readings 50
All rights reserved
ISSN 0305-814X
ISBN 0-255 36428-8

Many IEA publications are translated into languages other than
English or are reprinted. Permission to translate or to reprint should
be sought from the General Director at the address above.

Printed in Great Britain by
Hartington Fine Arts Limited, Lancing, West Sussex
Set in Times Roman 11.5 on 12 point

Contents

Introduction   *Professor Robert A. Mundell*   v

The Authors   vii

Purpose and Scope of the Paper   xi

Part 1: Alternative Exchange Rate Arrangements   1

Table 1: Alternative Exchange Rate Arrangements   2

Part 2: The Evolution of the International Monetary System   5

1870–1914: The Classical Gold Standard   5

1925–1937: The Interwar Gold Standard   6

1945–1973: The Bretton Woods System   7

1973–1998: Floating Exchange Rates   9

Towards European Monetary Unification   10

Part 3: The History of Monetary Unions   11

National Monetary Unions   12

Multinational Monetary Unions   23

Other Monetary Unions   30

Why are Monetary Unions Created and Dissolved?   32

Table 2: Dissolution of Some Monetary Unions in the 20th Century   33

Part 4: Lessons for EMU from the History of Monetary Unions 35

Commentaries

Few 'Lessons from History' 41

Sir Samuel Brittan

The Euro and History Lessons 47

Lord Currie of Marylebone

Is EMU Sustainable without Political Union? 53

Dr Walter Eltis

EMU as a Monetary Order 59

Professor David Laidler

Must Political Union Accompany Monetary Union? 63

Professor Anna J. Schwartz

Putting the Cart before the Horse 69

Sir Alan Walters

Summary

Back Cover

INTRODUCTION

Robert A. Mundell

OVER MOST OF HISTORY, MONETARY UNIFICATION HAS FOLLOWED POLITICAL INTEGRATION. This is for several reasons, the most important of which is that the monetary system is an expression of national sovereignty and, when money is overvalued, a fiscal resource of the first magnitude.

Most of our historical examples of monetary integration between independent countries concern metallic currencies for the simple reason that metals have been at the base of monetary systems for nearly all of recorded history. Countries that used the same metal as their currency unit achieved monetary integration. Under the gold and silver standards, currencies were just names for different quantities of the precious metals.

European Monetary Union differs from both the examples. Although an increased degree of political integration is generally thought to be a necessary accompaniment of integration, EMU has proceeded thus far without political integration. On the other hand, because the euro is based on paper and book-keeping currency, it differs from silver and gold standards or bimetallism. Monetary integration is more difficult with overvalued paper currencies than with metallic currencies that exchange along the principles of free coinage.

What makes a successful international currency? Elsewhere I have discussed several factors that in history have made drachmas and staters, denarii and aurei, dinars and dirhems, ducats and soldi, guilders and stivers, louis' and ecus, pounds and shillings, dollars and cents, great currencies in the past. The list includes size of transactions domain, stability of policy, absence of controls, fall-back value, a sense of permanence, low interest rates and a strong central state.

The euro fares well in these categories except fall-back value and strong central state. But in the modern system, large gold and foreign exchange reserves compensate for lack of fall-back value; and the existence of Nato as a security umbrella for the EU goes far to correct its current weakness as a 'strong central state'. At the same time it suggests the imperative of increased political integration in the Union.

The history of monetary unions is a valuable source of knowledge about the prospects for the European Monetary Union, even if the lessons of history are not always straightforward. I welcome this contribution by Michael D. Bordo and Lars Jonung as a thought-provoking analysis of what history may teach us about the future of European monetary unification.

Robert Mundell
C. Lowell Harriss Professor of Economics
Columbia University
Nobel Laureate in Economics, 1999

January 2000

Editor's Note

In Readings 50, as in all IEA publications, the views expressed are those of the authors not of the Institute (which has no corporate view), its Trustees, Advisers or Directors.

THE AUTHORS

Michael D. Bordo is a professor at Rutgers University, New Jersey. His research, mainly in monetary history, is focused on the gold standard, the Bretton Woods system and financial crises. He is a consultant at the International Monetary Fund and at the Federal Reserve Bank of St Louis. He has published several books, most recently *Essays on the Gold Standard and Related Regimes* (Cambridge University Press) and, as editor, several volumes on the international monetary system, including *The Classical Gold Standard in Retrospective* (with Anna Schwartz) and *A Retrospective on the Bretton Woods System* (with Barry Eichengreen).

Lars Jonung is a professor at the Stockholm School of Economics. His research is focused on Swedish stabilisation policy, particularly on the policy of the Riksbank, and on the history of economic thought. He has participated in the SNS Economic Policy Group, most recently in the 1996 report where he provided the section on EMU. He was economic advisor to the Skandinaviska Enskilda Banken in 1989–91 and chief economic adviser to the Swedish prime minister, Carl Bildt, in 1992–94. He has published several books, including *The Political Economy of Price Controls: The Swedish Experience 1970–1985* and, as editor, *The Stockholm School of Economics Revisited* among others.

Bordo and Jonung have co-authored several articles, as well as *The Long-Run Behaviour of Velocity: The International Evidence*. They are presently working on a study of the evolution of stabilisation policies.

Samuel Brittan is a columnist at the Financial Times. His most recent books are *Capitalism With a Human Face* (Edward Elgar – 1995, Fontana – 1996) and *Essays, Moral, Political and Economic* (Edinburgh University Press 1998). He is an Honorary Fellow of Jesus College, Cambridge; an Hon. Doctor of Letters (Heriot-Watt University, Edinburgh): an Hon. Doctor of the University of Essex. He has been awarded the George Orwell, Senior Harold Wincott and Ludwig Erhard prizes. He was knighted in 1993 for 'services to economic journalism' and also became that year a Chevalier de la Legion d'Honneur.

David Currie (Lord Currie of Marylebone) is Deputy Dean of External Relations, Director of the Regulation Initiative and Professor of Economics at London Business School. His research interests are in international macroeconomics and policy and in government regulation of industry. He has served on a variety of UK government advisory bodies including the Treasury's Panel of Independent Forecasters (the "Wise Men") and the Retail Price Index Advisory Committee. His recent books include *Policy Rules, Credibility and International Macroeconomic Policy* (1994), *North-South Linkages and International Macroeconomic Policy* (1995), *The Pros and Cons of EMU* (1997) and *Will the Euro Work?* (1998).

Walter Eltis is an Emeritus Fellow of Exeter College, Oxford and Visiting Professor of Economics in the University of Reading. He is co-author with Robert Bacon of *Britain's Economic Problem: Too Few Producers*, and author of *Britain, Europe and EMU* (Macmillan 2000). His other books include *The Classical Theory of Economic Growth* (1984). From 1992 to 1995 he was Chief Economic Adviser to the President of the Board of Trade, and from 1986 to 1992 Economic Director and subsequently Director General of the National Economic Development Office.

David Laidler has been Professor of Economics at the University of Western Ontario since 1975. Before coming to Canada in 1975, he taught at the University of California, Berkeley (Assistant Professor 1963–66), the University of Essex (Lecturer 1966–69) and the University of Manchester (Professor 1969–75). In 1972, he was the British Association for the Advancement of Science's Lister Lecturer, and in 1982, he was elected to the Royal Society of Canada.

A specialist in monetary economics and its history, Professor Laidler has written numerous academic books and articles. His latest book is *Fabricating the Keynesian Revolution: Studies of the Inter-War Literature on Money, the Cycle and Unemployment* published by Cambridge University Press in 1999.

Anna J. Schwartz, a member of the research staff of the National Bureau of Economic Research, is a Distinguished Fellow of the American Economic Association, and an Honorary Fellow of the Institute of Economic Affairs. She is co-author with Milton Friedman of *A Monetary History of the United States* and other studies of monetary economics. A collection of her articles, *Money in Historical Perspective*, was published in 1987 by the University of Chicago Press.

Alan Walters has been Vice Chairman and Director of AIG Trading Group since 1991. He was Chief Economic Adviser to the Prime Minister 1981–84 and 1989. He has been Professor of Econometrics at the University of Birmingham and Professor of Economics at the London School of Economics and Johns Hopkins University. He has contributed widely to the learned journals and he has written books *inter alia* on econometrics, transport economics, monetary economics and development economics. He was knighted in 1983.

PURPOSE AND SCOPE
OF THE PAPER

THE CURRENT PROCESS OF CREATING EUROPEAN MONETARY UNION (EMU)[1] and the European Central Bank (ECB) has contributed to an interest in the establishment, performance and demise of monetary or currency unions. Monetary history, properly interpreted, may shed light on a number of issues in the present debate on a common European currency. The purpose of this paper is to examine the record of monetary unions to extract such lessons.[2]

First, we briefly review alternative exchange rate arrangements that have evolved in the past two centuries to give a background to our history of monetary unions. Next, we look at the establishment and performance of a small number of monetary unions. We make a distinction between national and multinational monetary unions. We focus on three national monetary unions (the United States, Italy and Germany), and two multinational unions (the Latin Monetary Union and the Scandinavian Monetary Union). We conclude with a summary of the most important lessons from history that we want to draw from our account concerning the future of EMU.

---

[1] EMU is now often used as an abbreviation for 'economic and monetary union' in the European Union.

[2] The lack of interest in the history of monetary unions is surprising, given the present debate about EMU. We have found very few systematic studies of the history of monetary unions pertaining to EMU. T. Theurl *Eine gemeinsame Währung für Europa: 12 Lehren aus der Geschichte*, Innsbruck: Österreichischer Studien Verlag, 1992, and W. Vanthoor, *European Monetary Union since 1848: A Political and Historical Analysis*, Cheltenham: Edward Elgar, 1996, are exceptions, primarily based on an economic-historical perspective.

PART 1

ALTERNATIVE EXCHANGE RATE ARRANGEMENTS

EVERY COUNTRY WITH A CURRENCY OF ITS OWN faces the problem of setting its exchange rate arrangement. This choice has both a domestic and an international aspect. The domestic aspect pertains to the monetary arrangements which determine the domestic money supply. The international aspect relates to the monetary arrangements between countries. Two basic types of exchange rate arrangements exist – fixed and flexible exchange rates – along with a number of intermediate variants including adjustable pegs and managed floating systems.

In convertible régimes, if a number of countries define their currencies in terms of the same precious metal, for example gold, then they would adhere to a fixed exchange rate. If countries define their monies in terms of different metals, for example some in gold and some in silver, then their exchange rates would float. Under a fiat system, nations could follow either fixed or floating rates.

History demonstrates the emergence of a number of exchange rate arrangements summarised in Table 1 under three headings. Under the *first* heading are irrevocably fixed exchange rates in the form of monetary unions – an extreme form of a fixed exchange rate system. Specie standards and currency boards are also included under the first heading. The *second* heading covers various types of pegged but adjustable rates like the Bretton Woods system and the ERM (the European Exchange Rate Mechanism). Finally, different monetary arrangements under floating or flexible rates are placed under the *third* heading.

As in a convertible system, countries following fiat money régimes can adhere to fixed exchange rates with each other. The key advantage of doing so is to avoid the transaction costs of exchange in international trade. However, a fixed rate system based on fiat money may not provide the stable nominal anchor of the specie convertibility

1

Table 1: Alternative Exchange Rate Arrangements

---

1 Truly (irrevocably) fixed exchange rate arrangements (with high credibility)
   (a) Monetary unions with a common currency (the US and EMU)
   (b) Commodity or specie standards (the gold standard)
   (c) Currency boards (Hong Kong, Argentina, Estonia)

2 Fixed but adjustable exchange rates (pegged rates)
   (a) The Bretton Woods system
   (b) Currency baskets
   (c) The ERM system

3 Floating exchange rates
   (a) Rule-based systems
       Price stabilisation (Knut Wicksell's norm)
       Wage stabilisation (David Davidson's norm)
       Monetary targeting
       Inflation targeting
       Other norms
   (b) Discretion-based systems
       Discretionary monetary standards

---

régime unless all the members define their currencies in terms of the currency of one dominant country, for example, the US under Bretton Woods or Germany in the European Monetary System (EMS). This country in turn follows a rule which requires it to maintain price stability. Alternatively, the members collectively formulate a mechanism such as creating an international central bank to ensure price stability.

In a fiat money flexible rate régime, the absence of the nominal anchor of the fixed price of specie opens up the possibility that monetary authorities, in order to satisfy the political goals of the government (for example, its fiscal demands or demands to maintain full employment) could use the printing press to engineer high inflation.

The theoretical literature concludes that it is difficult to provide an unambiguous ranking of exchange rate arrangements. Empirical evidence is thus crucial in assessing the performance of the various alternatives. Unfortunately, such studies do not give rise to clear conclusions either. It is still an open question as to which system leads to the 'best' result.[3]

The European Union (EU) has decided from the 'menu' of alternative exchange rate systems (Table 1) that the proper choice of exchange rate arrangement for its members is a monetary union. These plans for future monetary union in Europe are most easily understood as part of the evolution of the international monetary system.

---

3 Much of the discussion about which countries should form a monetary union has been framed within the context of the optimal currency area approach pioneered by R.A. Mundell, 'A Theory of Optimum Currency Areas', *American Economic Review*, Vol. 51, Nov. 1961, pp. 509–17. In spite of a great outpouring of this literature in recent years, it has not given rise to any clear policy conclusions.

PART 2

THE EVOLUTION OF THE INTERNATIONAL MONETARY SYSTEM

OUR CHRONOLOGICAL REVIEW of the history of the international monetary system starts with the rise of the gold standard. This system dominated international monetary arrangements from the second half of the 19th century until the early 1970s. The roots of EMU can be traced back to the Bretton Woods system, the last truly international monetary system based on the gold standard.

1870–1914: The Classical Gold Standard

In the 1870s the world switched from bimetallism to gold monometallism. Some researchers argue that it was primarily the result of political motives – nations wished to emulate the example of Britain, the world's leading commercial and industrial power, which had based its exchange rates on gold since the early 18th century. A monetary system based on gold was regarded as a prerequisite for commercial and economic progress. When Germany used the Franco-Prussian War indemnity to finance the creation of a gold standard, other prominent European nations followed. Sweden, Denmark and Norway went jointly on gold as part of the Scandinavian monetary union established in the 1870s. The classical gold standard evolved from domestic standards by the common fixing of gold prices by member nations. Unlike later arrangements, the classical gold standard was not constructed and regulated by international agreements.

Central banks played an important rôle in the classical gold standard. By varying their discount rates and using other tools of monetary policy, they were supposed to follow 'the rules of the game' and speed up adjustment to balance of payments disequilibria. Actually, many central banks violated the rules by not raising their discount rates or by using 'gold devices' which artificially altered the price of gold in the face of a deficit. But the violations were never sufficient to threaten convertibility. They were tolerated because market participants viewed them as temporary attempts by central banks to smooth interest rates and economic activity, keeping within the overriding constraint of convertibility.

Although the gold standard operated very smoothly for close to four decades, the episode was punctuated by periodic financial crises. In most cases when faced with both an internal and an external drain, the Bank of England and other European central banks followed Bagehot's rule of lending freely but at a penalty rate. On several occasions, for example in 1890 and again in 1907, even the Bank of England's commitment to convertibility was put to the test, and cooperation with the Banque de France and other central banks was required to save it. The cooperation that did occur was spasmodic and was not an integral part of the operation of the classical gold standard. More importantly, during periods of financial crisis, private capital flows aided the Bank. Such stabilising capital movements most likely reflected market participants' belief in the credibility of Britain's commitment to maintain gold convertibility of the British pound.

By the beginning of World War One, the gold standard had evolved into a gold exchange standard. In addition to substituting fiduciary national monies for gold to economise on scarce gold reserves, many countries also held convertible foreign exchange (mainly deposits in London). Thus the system evolved into a massive pyramid of credit built upon a tiny base of gold. The possibility of a confidence crisis, triggering a collapse of the system, increased as the gold reserves at the centre diminished. The advent of World War One triggered such a collapse as the belligerents scrambled to convert their outstanding foreign liabilities into gold. Although the gold standard was reinstated in two variants later in the twentieth century, the world discovered that, like Humpty Dumpty of the famous nursery rhyme, it could never be put back together again.

1925–1937: The Interwar Gold Standard

The gold standard was reinstated after World War One as a gold exchange standard. Britain and other countries, alarmed by the postwar experience of inflation and exchange rate instability, were eager to return to the prewar halcyon days of gold convertibility. The system reestablished in 1925 was an attempt to restore the old régime but to economise on gold in the face of a perceived gold shortage. Based on principles developed at the Genoa Conference in

1922, members were encouraged to adopt central bank statutes that substituted foreign exchange for gold reserves and discouraged gold holdings by the private sector. The new system only lasted for six years, crumbling because of several fatal flaws in its structure after Britain's departure from the gold standard in September 1931.

After the collapse of the gold exchange standard throughout the world in the 1930s, there was a retreat towards autarky which included trade restrictions, exchange controls and bilateralism. The planning that led to the establishment of the Bretton Woods system aimed to avoid these evils.

A strong argument made for fixed exchange rates in the European monetary system (EMS) was based on the perception that the devaluations that occurred in the 1930s, beginning with the devaluation of the pound in 1931, were competitive ('beggar thy neighbour'), involving considerable overshooting because of the destabilising nature of short term capital flows. However, in a number of cases, when devaluation was accompanied by an expansionary monetary policy, world trade actually increased.

1945–1973: The Bretton Woods System

Bretton Woods, as a convertible global monetary régime, should be viewed within the context of the gold standard because the United States (the most important commercial power) defined its parity in terms of gold and all other members defined their parities in terms of dollars. The Articles of Agreement signed at Bretton Woods, New Hampshire, in 1944 represented a compromise between American and British plans. They combined the flexibility and freedom for policy makers of a floating rate system which the British team wanted, with the nominal stability of the gold standard rule emphasised by the US. The system established involved pegged exchange rates but members could alter their parities in the face of a fundamental disequilibrium. Members were encouraged to use domestic stabilisation policies to offset temporary disturbances, and they were protected from speculative attack by capital controls. The International Monetary Fund was to provide temporary liquidity assistance and to oversee the operation of the system.

Besides being based on the principle of convertibility with the US rather than Britain as the dominant country, Bretton Woods differed from the classical gold standard in a number of other fundamental ways. *First*, it was an arrangement mandated by an international

7

agreement between governments, whereas the gold standard evolved more informally. *Second*, domestic policy autonomy was encouraged even at the expense of convertibility – in sharp contrast to the gold standard where convertibility was the key feature. *Third*, and most important, capital movements were suppressed by controls.

The Bretton Woods system, in its convertible phase from 1959 to 1971, was characterised by exceptional macroeconomic performance for the advanced countries. It had the lowest and most stable inflation rate and the highest and most stable real growth rates of any modern monetary régime.[4] Moreover, it faced smaller demand and supply shocks than under the gold standard. However, it was short-lived, suggesting that the reason for its brief existence was not the external environment but, like the gold exchange standard, structural flaws in the régime.

The flaws of Bretton Woods echoed those of the gold exchange standard. Adjustment was inadequate, prices were downwardly inflexible and declining output was prevented by expansionary economic policy. Under the rules the exchange rate could be altered but, in practice, it rarely was because of the fear of overwhelming speculative pressure, which in turn reflected market beliefs that governments would not follow the policies necessary to maintain convertibility. Hence, the system in its early years was propped up by capital controls and in its later years by cooperation among the leading industrial countries (the G-10). As a substitute for scarce gold, the system relied increasingly on US dollars generated by persistent US payments deficits. The resultant asymmetry between the US and the rest of the world was resented by the French. The confidence problem was the growing risk of a run on US gold reserves as outstanding dollar liabilities increased relative to gold reserves.

The Bretton Woods system collapsed between 1968 and 1971. The United States broke the implicit rules of the dollar standard by not maintaining price stability. The rest of the world did not want to absorb additional dollars for fear of rising inflation. Surplus countries (especially Germany) were reluctant to revalue.

Another important source of strain on the system was the unworkability of the adjustable peg in the context of increasing capital

---

[4]   See, for example, M.D. Bordo, 'The Bretton Woods International Monetary System: An Historical Overview', in M.D. Bordo and B. Eichengreen (eds.), *A Retrospective on the Bretton Woods System*, Chicago: University of Chicago Press, 1993, pp. 3–108.

mobility. Speculation against a fixed parity could not be stopped by either traditional policies or international rescue packages. The Americans were forced by British and French decisions in the summer of 1971 to convert dollars into gold. The impasse was ended by President Richard Nixon's closing of the 'gold window' on 15 August 1971.

In conclusion, under the Bretton Woods system gold still served as a nominal anchor. This link to gold was important in constraining US monetary policy (at least until the mid 1960s) and in turn the monetary policy of the rest of the world. This may explain the low inflation rates and the low degree of inflation persistence observed in the 1950s and 1960s. However, credibility was considerably weaker than under the classical gold standard, making the dollar-gold standard less effective as a nominal anchor. Moreover, when US domestic interests clashed with convertibility of the dollar into gold, the anchor was stretched and then jettisoned. This was evident in the US reduction and subsequent removal of gold reserve requirements in 1965, the closing of first the Gold Pool in 1968 and then the gold window itself in 1971. This step marked the demise of gold in the international monetary system.

1973–2000: Floating Exchange Rates

As a reaction to the flaws of the Bretton Woods system, the world turned to generalised floating exchange rates in March 1973. Though the early years of the floating exchange rate were often characterised as a 'dirty float', whereby monetary authorities extensively intervened to affect both the levels of volatility and exchange rates, by the end of the 1970s it evolved into a system where exchange market intervention occurred primarily to smooth out fluctuations. Again in the 1980s exchange market intervention was used by the Group of Seven countries as part of a strategy of policy coordination. In recent years, floating exchange rates have been assailed from many quarters for excessive volatility in both nominal and real exchange rates, which in turn increase macroeconomic instability and raise the costs of international transactions.

There have been many perceived problems, including the ability or otherwise of the flexible régime to accommodate the effects of the massive oil price shocks in the 1970s and other shocks in subsequent years without significant disruption, as well as the perception that pegged exchange rate arrangements amongst major countries are

9

doomed to failure. Nevertheless, the prospects for significant reform of the present system seem remote.

The advent of general floating in 1973 and its longevity suggest that the lessons of Bretton Woods have been well learned. Major countries like the United States are not willing to subject their domestic policy autonomy to that of another country whose commitment they cannot be sure of, nor to a supranational monetary authority they cannot control. The key advantage of floating – the freedom to pursue an independent monetary policy – still holds good today, at least for major countries.

Towards European Monetary Unification

Since the breakdown of the Bretton Woods system, Europe has been moving steadily towards creating a monetary union with perfectly fixed exchange rates. This reflects the desire of the member countries of the EU for economic and political integration. On the road to that end, the ERM within the EMS, established in 1979, was modelled on Bretton Woods, although it was not based on gold and it incorporated flexibility and greater financial resources. It appeared successful in the late 1980s when member countries followed policies similar to Germany, the centre country. It then broke down in 1992–93, in a manner similar to the collapse of the Bretton Woods system in 1968–71 and for similar reasons – because pegged exchange rates, capital mobility and policy autonomy do not mix. It collapsed in the face of massive speculative pressure on countries, regardless of whether they were following policies inconsistent with their pegs to Germany or seemingly following the rules, whose ultimate commitment to the peg was doubted by the agents in financial markets in the face of rising unemployment.

After the monetary collapse of 1992–93, which represented a temporary setback for EMU, the unification process has continued; eleven countries have now adopted a single currency, the euro, and are bound together in economic and monetary union.

PART 3

THE HISTORY OF
MONETARY UNIONS

A MONETARY UNION OR A UNIFIED CURRENCY AREA is the extreme version of a fixed exchange rate monetary régime (see Table 1, page 2). The essence of a monetary union is that all the member states or entities adopt the same currency as a unit of account, medium of exchange and store of value: the monetary union therefore has one exchange rate towards the rest of the world.

The history of monetary unions is most easily understood if we make a distinction between national monetary unions and multinational monetary unions. By a national monetary union we mean that political and monetary sovereignty go hand in hand. Roughly speaking, the borders of the nation-state are the borders of the monetary area. For example, within the British monetary union comprising England, Scotland, Wales and Northern Ireland, Scottish and Northern Irish commercial banks still issue bank notes. These notes are perfectly interchangeable with Bank of England notes. Likewise, in the United States each of the Federal Reserve Banks issues dollar bills perfectly acceptable in every reserve district – a 5-dollar bill issued by the Federal Reserve Bank of Richmond is always interchangeable with a 5-dollar bill from any of the other Federal Reserve Banks. A national monetary union has as a rule only one monetary authority, commonly a central bank.

By a multinational monetary union we mean international monetary cooperation between a number of independent countries based on permanently fixed exchange rates between their currencies. Multinational monetary unions occur when independent nation-states link their monies together through a perfectly fixed exchange rate, so that one country's money is perfectly exchangeable for another member country's at a fixed price. Indeed, an extreme example of this would be that all the member states use the same currency. There is as a rule no common monetary authority in a multinational monetary union. An example of such a union is the Scandinavian monetary union which had one common currency, the Scandinavian *krona*, and three members: the countries of Sweden, Norway and Denmark. Each member maintained its own central bank.

It is important to stress the distinction between the monetary union *per se* and the type of monetary policy pursued within the union. Adoption of a common currency by member states can be consistent with alternative sets of institutional arrangements governing monetary policy, ranging from complete *laissez-faire* to monolithic central banking. This distinction will be illustrated in the following account, showing that monetary unions, once created, differed substantially depending on the evolution of monetary institutions or arrangements. The currencies could be unified without specifying any particular rule for governing monetary policy, as seen from the following account which focuses on three national monetary unions, the US, the Italian and the German, and two multinational monetary unions, the Latin and the Scandinavian. We deal here primarily with the monetary experience of the late 18th and the 19th centuries.

National Monetary Unions

The United States Monetary Union[5]

Since all of the colonies were founded, chartered and, to some extent, administered by the British government, their monetary systems were strongly influenced by British monetary regulations and practices. The principal medium of exchange in the colonies, as in England, was silver coins denominated in pounds, shillings and pence. No banks in the modern sense existed, so there were no deposits or bank notes. One problem from the outset was that the British Navigation Acts discouraged the export from Britain of British silver coins and the colonies were also prohibited from setting up their own mints. Consequently, the bulk of coins used were Spanish silver coins,

---

[5] The account of US monetary unification is based on the following works: B.T. McCallum, 'Money and Prices in Colonial America: A New Test of Competing Theories', *Journal of Political Economy*, Vol. 100, 1992, pp. 143–61; E.J. Perkins, *American Public Finance and Financial Services, 1700–1815*, Columbus, Oh.: Ohio State University Press, 1994; A.J. Rolnick, B.D. Smith and W.E. Weber, 'The Origins of the Monetary Union in the United States', in P. Siklos (ed.), *Varieties of Monetary Experiences*, Boston, Mass.: Kluwer, 1994; and A. Fraas, 'The Second Bank of the United States: An Instrument for Interregional Monetary Union', *Journal of Economic History*, Vol. 34, 1974, pp. 427–46.

called 'pieces of eight' or 'dollars'. All of the colonies throughout the 17th and 18th centuries complained of a perennial 'shortage' of silver. This may have reflected the tendency of developing countries to run chronic balance of payments deficits. It may also have reflected deterioration in the quality of Spanish silver coins in an era before modern milling and minting techniques had been invented.

To counteract this shortage of specie, which was commonly believed to be a deterrent to continuous growth and prosperity, colonial governments resorted to a number of techniques. One was a legal declaration that an ounce of silver in a specified coin was worth more shillings in the colony in question than elsewhere, which was equivalent to a modern devaluation. This practice was prohibited by the English government in 1692. A second device was the use of commodity money.

A third device, and the one most commonly used, was the issue of paper money in one of two forms: land bank bills, which were IOUs based on the security of mortgages, and bills of credit (notes issued by the colonial government promising to repay the holder in specie at some future date based on the collection of taxes). These bills were freely transferable without endorsement from holder to holder, were issued in convenient denominations and were printed in a form somewhat similar to today's money. These bills of credit came quickly to be accepted as a medium of exchange and served as a major form of colonial currency.

In the first half of the eighteenth century, the New England colonies as well as South Carolina issued sufficient amounts of paper monies to displace all specie from the money supply and hence force the colonies off the fixed exchange rate specie standard. This led to rapid inflation and depreciating exchange rates. Other colonies (most notably the Middle Atlantic states) did not issue enough paper money to displace specie and hence they experienced low inflation and stable exchange rates.

In reaction to the New England experience of high inflation from 1720 to 1750, the British Board of Trade imposed the Currency Act of 1751 prohibiting those colonies from issuing bills of credit not fully backed by specie. The prohibition on paper money issue was extended to the other colonies in 1764 – although it was not universally implemented.

The American War of Independence (1776–1783) was largely financed by the issue of fiat money both by the Congress (the continentals) and by the States (bills of credit). Paper money was issued at the rate of 50 per cent per annum in the first five years of the war, generating rapid inflation of over 65 per cent per annum and rapid depreciation of the exchange rate. The inflation ended after a currency reform in 1780 under which the federal government stopped issuing bills of credit and the states agreed to accept outstanding bills in payment of taxes at 40 dollars to 1 in specie (a value much lower than the exchange rate of 1780) until 1783, after which date the continental would become worthless.

After the war, during the Confederation period (1783–89), the States continued to issue bills of credit, some of which were credibly backed by future taxes and some of which were not. Consequently, problems similar to those of the colonial era reemerged, namely excessive volatility of exchange rates leading to exchange rate risk, high transactions costs and competitive seigniorage.

The US monetary union was created with the signing of the Constitution in 1789. The constitution gave the Congress the sole power to 'coin money' and 'regulate the value thereof'. Moreover, the Coinage Act of 1792 defined the US dollar in terms of fixed weights of gold and silver coins, placing the country on a bimetallic standard. Finally, establishment of a national mint in Philadelphia in 1792 secured the foundations for an effective currency area.

While the Congress was given the exclusive power to coin money, the States were allowed to charter commercial banks and to regulate their note-issuing activity. All bank notes had to be convertible into specie. In the early decades of the 19th century, bank note issue varied considerably and some bank notes circulated at a discount. Moreover, there is evidence that the price level may have been higher in the West than in the East.

The movement to a complete monetary union with a more uniform nationwide price level was aided by the practices of the First Bank of the United States (1791–1811) and the Second Bank of the United States (1816–1836). Neither Bank was designed as a modern central bank but as a public bank. Both banks were sufficiently well capitalised to be able to provide the government with medium-term bridge loans to finance shortfalls in government tax receipts. Both were also intended to provide loans to the private sector to encourage economic development. Finally, it was deemed imperative that they hold sufficient specie reserves always to maintain convertibility of their notes. One of the practices of both Banks was to enforce the convertibility of state bank note issues and to transfer specie between regions.

After the demise of the Second Bank of the United States in 1836, the United States did not have any form of central bank until the establishment of the Federal Reserve System in 1914. However, the US Treasury served as a monetary authority and maintained specie convertibility. Although the 19th century was characterised by considerable banking instability, the monetary union remained intact with the exception of the Civil War period (1861–65) when the Confederate States issued their own fiat currency. During the Civil War the Confederacy issued its own fiduciary inconvertible currency denominated in dollars. In the face of great difficulties in raising tax revenues and in selling debt both at home and abroad, the Confederate government expanded its money issues at an ever-increasing rate. By the end of the Civil War hyperinflation had vastly reduced the value of Confederate notes. Upon Union victory in April 1865, Confederate notes were declared illegal in the United States.[6] Monetary unification of the US was thus not finalised until long after political unification.

The Italian Monetary Union[7]

The main reason for the establishment of a currency union on the Apennine peninsula in the 1860s was political unification of the area now known as Italy.[8] The unification process, led by the Kingdom of Sardinia, was completed in 1861. Previously financial matters had been handled in a widely disparate manner in the various small Italian states. In 1859, as many as 90 different metallic currencies were legal

---

6   E.M. Lerner, 'Inflation in the Confederacy, 1861–65', in M. Friedman (ed.), *Studies in the Quantity Theory of Money*, Chicago: University of Chicago Press, 1956, 164–75.

7   The account of the monetary unification of Italy is based on contributions by M. Fratianni and F. Spinelli, 'Currency Competition, Fiscal Policy and the Money Supply Process in Italy from Unification to World War One', *Journal of European Economic History*, Vol. 14, No. 3, 1985, pp. 471–99; and V. Sannucci, 'The Establishment of a Central Bank: Italy in the Nineteenth Century', in M. De Cecco and A. Giovanni (eds.), *A European Central Bank*, Cambridge: Cambridge University Press, 1989, pp. 244–80.

8   Venetia was incorporated in 1866 after Italy had participated on the Prussian side in her war against Austria. The Papal States were incorporated in 1870 when France, who until then had acted as a protector of the sovereignty of the Papal States, was engaged in war with Prussia.

tender. In addition, major banks in the small states issued bank notes that served as legal tender in their respective regions. The vast number of different currencies was commonly regarded as a barrier to trade. In order to achieve more than a *de jure* unified Italy, measures were taken to turn the country into a monetary union as well.

The issue of coins was quickly resolved. During a brief transition period, four currencies were accepted while all other old currencies were exchanged into these. Finally, in 1862 a new, unified coinage system was introduced based on the lira of Sardinia. All pre-unification coins and paper monies were abolished and exchanged for coins denominated in the new lira, equal in value to the French franc. A bimetallic currency standard was preferred, primarily to conform to the monetary system of Italy's major trading partners and to accommodate the dominance of silver coins in southern Italy.[9] The currency ratio between silver and gold was set at the European standard of 15.5:1. When Italy introduced the lira, the price of gold was falling, creating a shortage of silver coins. The legislators acted by lowering the silver content of coins to 83.5 per cent instead of the customary 90 per cent. This led to an export of silver coins, a phenomenon that was enhanced by the suspension of convertibility a few years later.[10]

No immediate action was taken to establish a single monetary authority. Several regional banks were issuing notes as well as performing central bank functions. The Banca Nazionale nel Regno d'Italia (BNR) (which was formed by merging the previous national bank of Sardinia with some other state banks) held a leading position among banks, partly because it was the largest bank in operation and partly because it was the bank of the state that had led the political unification process.

Italian monetary research does not clearly explain why a single monetary authority was not created after unification. Apparently it was not the result of opposition to monetary unification. Given that Sardinia imposed her system on the rest of the country in a wide range of areas, neglecting the preferences of other states, it seems unlikely that she would have backed down if she wanted to establish

---

[9] See also the section on the Latin Monetary Union (below, pp. 23–26).

[10] For an account of the fineness of coins, see the section on the Latin Monetary Union (below, pp. 23–26).

the BNR as the central bank of Italy. Several explanations have been put forward. One suggests that it was simply a result of the general belief at the time that banking was like any other industry. Consequently, Italy would gain from competition between issuing banks, just as competition in other industries was considered to enrich the economy. Another possible explanation is that, prior to unification, regional commercial banks were credit institutions as well as note issuers. The general concept of Italian banking of the time was to combine these two functions: money was created in the form of bank notes in response to demands for credit. The central government may have concluded that the creation of one central bank would have destroyed, or severely impaired, the functioning of commercial banks at the local level and that the costs of this would exceed the benefits of control of the supply of paper money by a central bank.

When Italian monetary unification took place in 1862, almost the entire money stock consisted of coins. Since the supply of coinage was regulated by the supply of gold and silver, the fluctuations in the Italian money stock followed the international pattern. The share of coins in the money supply remained stable until the mid-1860s, indicating that, as long as bank notes were convertible into specie, the multiplicity of issuing banks did not create a problem.

The government's fiscal deficit rose sharply in the first half of the 1860s, worsening the strain already put on public finances by the central government assuming responsibility for the debt of the previous states. Italian bond prices fell abroad which drove specie out of Italy, leaving the reserves of the commercial banks dangerously low and restricting their ability to lend to the government. To come to terms with the new situation, the government declared bank notes inconvertible into specie in 1866, *corso forzoso* in the language of the day.[11] Subsequently, the government received a large loan in notes from the BNR in return for strengthening the position of the BNR. The notes of other banks were made legal tender and at the same time convertible into BNR notes. The latter, however, were not convertible into other banks' notes. Consequently, BNR notes served as reserves for other banks.

The Italian money stock rose by 29 per cent in 1866 and by 9 per cent in 1867, producing a depreciation of the lira. The arrangement

---

[11] *Corso forzoso* can be broadly translated as 'forced circulation'.

with BNR notes as reserves provided the government with an instrument to control the money supply and was initially successful in lowering inflation and increasing the value of the lira. As the government deficit rose again, however, the money supply was once more allowed to rise. Furthermore, the issuing and inconvertibility of paper money drove coins out of the country. The ensuing shortage of small denomination coins led many smaller banks to put notes into circulation illegally. These developments led to legislation in 1874 stating that the remaining six currency-issuing banks held the right to print legal tender bank notes, the volume being restricted by the government.[12]

The *corso forzoso* was ended in 1884. Convertibility was resumed and the lira returned to gold parity. The notes of the six remaining note-issuing banks could be exchanged for each other on a one-to-one basis, although the parity was not stipulated by law. As a consequence of the *de facto* fixed exchange rate between the notes, any bank had an incentive to increase its stock of notes. The risk of the government discovering an over-issue was small. Furthermore, deteriorating government finances increased the likelihood that any illegal over-issue of notes would be legalised.

In 1891, a liquidity crisis resulting from the low levels of reserves relative to outstanding notes was pending. The government, as expected, responded by legalising the total volume of notes in circulation by lowering the reserve requirements. An ensuing enquiry into the state of the banking system completed in 1893 led to a major restructuring of the system. The Banca d'Italia was formed by amalgamating the BNR and the two remaining note-issuing Tuscan banks. The three remaining note-issuing banks were put under direct state supervision.[13] Despite these measures, specie continued to flow out of Italy. The lira depreciated, mainly as a result of the failure to reduce the excess issue of notes. The outflow triggered yet another liquidity crisis. In 1894, bank notes once again were declared inconvertible into specie.

---

[12] The six banks were the BNR; the southern banks, Banco di Napoli and Banco di Sicilia; the Banca Romana (previously the bank of the Papal States); Banca Nazionale Toscana; and Banca Toscana di Credito.

[13] They were the newly created Banca d'Italia, the Banca di Napoli and the Banca di Sicilia. The Banca Romana went into liquidation in 1893. Its business was taken over by the BNR.

As part of the 1893 reshaping of the banking system, the government and the banks agreed to restrict the note issue to three times the volume of specie. In the long run this proved successful. The success was in no small part because the Banca d'Italia was established as the leading note-issuer with 75 per cent of total circulation. Fiscal discipline contributed to making the period until World War One one of monetary stability with an appreciating lira.

The formation of the Italian monetary union (like the formation of the US monetary union) took place after political unification and it was a time-consuming process.

The German Monetary Union

The German monetary – as well as political – unification process proceeded stepwise. Scholars do not agree when the most important step towards monetary unification occurred. Holtfrerich (1993) suggests that the unification of coinage in 1857 represents the major, though not the final move towards a monetary union.[14] Others like Kindleberger claim that the creation of the Reichsbank in 1875 was the most important step. The disagreement has important implications:[15] in the former case monetary unification preceded political unification and in the latter the order was reversed. We are of the opinion that the most important step towards monetary unification was taken after the establishment of the Reich.

Prior to German monetary unification, each principality and free town issued its own coins and, in some cases, paper money. Since many of the principalities were quite small, it was inevitable that their coins spread across their borders as an accompaniment to the free flow of migration within the *Deutscher Bund*. In addition, many foreign coins, not least of French origin, circulated within Germany. Money exchanges were common and profitable.

The diversity of coins was perceived as a great nuisance. Merchants and industrialists, often with a liberal orientation, became the main proponents of unified economic and monetary conditions to reduce transaction costs emanating from the monetary disarray, while

---

[14] C.-L. Holtfrerich, 'Did Monetary Unification Precede or Follow Political Unification of Germany in the 19th Century?', *European Economic Review*, Vol. 37, 1993, pp. 518–24.

[15] C.P. Kindleberger, *A Financial History of Western Europe*, London: George Allen & Unwin, 1981.

the governments of the principalities resisted, safeguarding their seigniorage gains.

In 1834, all internal customs barriers were removed. This agreement, known as the *Zollverein*, also proposed that the various coinage systems be integrated into a common standard. At that time, Germany could be divided roughly into two areas, each using the same unit of account and, apart from Bremen, each operating on a silver standard.[16] The southern states were the first to respond to the spirit of the *Zollverein* by signing the Munich Coin Treaty in 1837. One year later, the statutes of this treaty became part of a more general agreement among all the states of the *Zollverein*, the Dresden Coinage Convention, which provided further standardisation. This treaty stipulated that each state had to choose between the Thaler, the unit of account of the north, and the Gulden, the unit of account of the south. Both the Thaler and the Gulden were explicitly linked to silver as well as to each other, with 1 Thaler valued at 1.75 Gulden. All member states were required to withdraw from circulation all coins that were not adapted to the new standard, whether because of wear and tear or debasement at the mint.

The Dresden Convention created a double currency standard virtually all over Germany. Some states, however, had not joined the *Zollverein* and did not participate in the convention.[17] Each state still retained the right to determine how to divide the currency into petty coins. In practice, following the Dresden treaty the Prussian 1-Thaler coin dominated the circulation throughout Germany, even gaining general acceptance in the southern regions that were on the Gulden standard.

The Vienna Coinage Treaty of 1857 constituted a further step towards monetary unification. The treaty incorporated Austria into the Dresden arrangement by fixing the exchange rate of 1 Thaler to 1.5 Austrian Gulden and to 1.75 south German Gulden.[18] The amount

---

[16] The two areas did not have a common currency, since the metal content of coins and system of fractional money differed across regions.

[17] These states included the cities of Bremen, Hamburg, and Lübeck, together with Schleswig-Holstein. They also included Austria and Liechtenstein that were to remain outside the unification process.

[18] Austria was subsequently forced to withdraw in 1867, following defeat in the war against Prussia.

of small-change coins that each state could issue was regulated. The old fractional coins issued at the beginning of the century were withdrawn. All existing 1-Thaler coins were granted legal tender status and every state was given the right to mint 1-Thaler *Vereinsmünzen*. Gulden coins and Thaler coins of other denominations remained legal tender in their respective regions. The new 1-Thaler *Vereinsmünze* was rapidly placed into circulation and almost completely overtook the Gulden.[19] The treaty also prohibited uncontrolled circulation of subsidiary coinage by limiting the amount each state could issue and by declaring subsidiary coins convertible into full-value coins. In effect, a system of double currencies was established.

Apart from the standardisation of the silver coin system, the Vienna Treaty included two major steps towards monetary unification. First, the circulation of gold coins, previously left to the discretion of each state, became subject to stringent rules. No gold coins other than special *Vereinshandelsgoldmünzen* designed for foreign trade were to be minted. The exchange of gold coins into silver at a fixed parity was forbidden as well, avoiding the risk of turning the currency standard into a bimetallic one. Second, the treaty dealt with paper money, the first international monetary arrangement ever to do so, by prohibiting the granting of legal tender status to inconvertible paper money.[20] The decision was aimed at Austria, where inconvertible notes had been issued since 1848. No measure was taken, however, to limit the circulation of convertible bank notes issued in several states. The demand for paper money (bank notes and state paper money) had grown primarily in the most industrialised regions of Germany. The number of note issuing banks rose to about 30 by the mid-1850s and the amount of notes in circulation grew rapidly.[21]

---

[19] C.-L. Holtfrerich, 'The Monetary Unification Process in Nineteenth-Century Germany: Relevance and Lessons for Europe Today', in M. De Cecco and A. Giovanni (eds.), *A European Central Bank*, *op. cit.*, p. 224, states that, prior to 1857, the south German states minted 90 per cent *Gulden* and 10 per cent *Vereinsmünze*, whereas after 1857 the relation was reversed.

[20] C.-L. Holtfrerich, 'The Monetary Unification Process in Nineteenth-Century Germany', *op. cit.*, p. 225.

[21] *Ibid.*, p. 228.

Although the coinage in Germany had been put on a common standard in 1857, voices were raised in the 1860s to continue the process of monetary unification. In 1870, the North German Federation, founded in 1867, prohibited new issues of state paper money and fixed the volume of note issues for most banks. These measures left the control of the future growth of paper money in the hands of the Prussian Bank.

The establishment in 1871 of the new unified German Reich, following the Franco-Prussian war, induced further steps. The Coinage Acts of 1871 and 1873 unified coinage throughout the Reich and introduced the Mark as the unit of account based on the decimal system. In order to link the German currency to the British pound, at the time the leading international currency, the gold standard was adopted with silver being relegated to use in coins of small denominations with less metal contents than their face values.[22] In 1875, a new banking act transformed the Prussian Bank into the Reichsbank and forced most other banks to opt for ordinary banking business.[23] The Reichsbank was to serve as the central bank for the new Germany. From the 1870s until the outbreak of World War One, Germany was part of the international gold standard. German monetary developments were determined by international developments. Money growth and prices moved in line with adherence to the gold standard.

Political unification epitomised by the creation of the German Reich was followed by three major changes in the German monetary system: the conversion of the currency standard from silver to gold, the replacement of the Thaler with the Mark as the unit of account and the formation of a single central bank that, in practice, monopolised the issuing of paper money. These changes meant that Germany, after a long process, was a fully fledged national monetary union. Monetary unification followed political unification.

---

[22] There was an exception to the rule, however, as outstanding silver Thalers remained legal tender.

[23] The termination of other banks' right to issue notes was not as straightforward as simply enacting a law forbidding it. Instead, the government opted to allow other state banks to carry on issuing notes but to stipulate stringent rules concerning the denominations of the notes and the total amount issued. Private banks were forced to choose between issuing notes valid only in the region of the bank or performing their business nationwide.

Multinational Monetary Unions

We deal here with two multinational monetary unions, the Latin and the Scandinavian monetary unions. These unions were based on a common coinage where each member country retained its central bank.

The Latin Monetary Union[24]

Prior to the establishment of the Latin Monetary Union, France, Belgium, Switzerland and, to some extent, Italy had a history of recognising each other's currencies as a means of payment. The basis of this arrangement was the French bimetallic system, in operation since 1803, which stipulated that the fineness of each coin, regardless of whether it was gold or silver, was to be 90 per cent and fixed the relative value of gold and silver at 15.5:1.

In the 1850s, a fall in the price of gold relative to the price of silver made gold coins overvalued at the mint. Consequently, it became profitable to melt silver coins and sell silver for gold at the market rate. As the price of gold continued to fall, even worn coins with low silver content started to disappear. The process left the countries virtually with a gold standard currency, since gold was the only medium of exchange that remained in circulation. However, the lack of silver coins meant a lack of small-denomination monies to use in minor transactions.

Switzerland was the first country to enact a feasible solution by reducing the silver content to 80 per cent in all coins except the 5-franc coin, thus ensuring that it was no longer profitable to export the new reduced-value silver coins. Switzerland also recognised that she was now, in effect, operating on a gold standard and in 1860 formally approved of gold as the basis of her currency.

Upon monetary unification, Italy decided to lower the silver content of every coin smaller than 1 franc to 83.5 per cent. The result of the actions of Italy and Switzerland was that mainly France but also Belgium were invaded by debased silver coins from their neighbouring countries which created seigniorage gains for the issuers.

---

[24] This section is based on M.L. Griffiths, 'Monetary Union in Europe: Lessons from the Nineteenth Century', Workshop Paper, Virginia Polytechnic Institute and State University, 1991, and A. Redish, 'The Latin Monetary Union and the Emergence of the International Gold Standard', in M.D. Bordo and F. Capie (eds.), *Monetary Regimes in Transition*, Cambridge: Cambridge University Press, 1993, chapter 3.

France reacted in 1864 by reducing the silver content in every silver coin, except the 5-franc coin, to Italy's level of 83.5 per cent and by suspending the acceptance of Swiss coins by her customs offices.

There was an apparent need for coordination. The acute shortage of small denomination coins constituted a hindrance to trade both within and between countries and forced the countries into remedial action. The unilateral response by each country of creating token coins of varying fineness created an additional problem in the form of one country reaping seigniorage benefits at the expense of the others. To deal with this situation Belgium proposed a joint monetary conference, held at the end of 1865, that created the Latin Monetary Union.

The main issues at the conference in 1865 were to secure and standardise the supply of subsidiary coinage for smaller transactions and the formal adoption of gold as the currency standard. The first issue was unanimously resolved by deciding that all silver coins of lesser value than the 5-franc coin were to be token coins with 83.5 per cent silver fineness which the state treasuries had to accept as payment up to 100 francs regardless of the country of origin. Each state treasury was then obliged to exchange the other state treasuries' holdings of its token coins into gold or silver 5-franc coins at par. The figure 83.5 per cent was chosen because of the dominant share of French and Italian token coins already in circulation compared to the amount of Swiss token coins. The total value of token coins that each country was permitted to mint was restricted to 6 francs per capita. As a result of strong French opposition and despite the fact that the other countries favoured such a move, the adoption of a gold standard was rejected in favour of retaining the bimetallic standard.[25]

The existing currencies continued to be in use virtually unchanged as parallel currencies. Each state treasury remained ultimately responsible for the redemption of its own coins. Apart from solving

---

[25] Two possible explanations for the French resistance have been put forward. One, mainly political, suggests that Napoleon III was planning a world monetary conference in 1867 where he hoped to be able to exchange a willingness to adopt the gold standard for a universal adoption of the French monetary standard. He was thus unwilling to convert to a gold standard at this stage. According to the other explanation, the Banque de France was concerned with redeeming the outstanding silver coins in gold. This would stretch the Bank's reserves to the limit and Napoleon III, dependent on the Bank for loans, had to follow the Bank on this account.

the problem of the scarcity of small-denomination coins, the purpose of the standardisation of the dimension and metal content of the coins was to eliminate the possibility of seigniorage gains through the minting of debased coins. While aiming to restrict the amount of money in circulation, the conference failed to consider restrictions preventing the member countries from issuing other forms of money – a failure that was to be exploited by the issue of paper notes. Consequently, the members still had considerable monetary independence.

Initially, the union achieved its aims. However, two problems soon emerged. After the inauguration of the union, the price of gold started to rise again, which led to silver 5-franc coins returning to circulation and gold coins being melted down or exported. At the same time, France and Italy began to issue inconvertible paper money. In the case of France, it was a temporary measure because of the war with Germany in 1870–71. Italy's chronic government deficit preserved inconvertibility of the lira until 1881 and then introduced it again in 1894. The increased money supply in Italy led to a depreciation of the lira. Consequently, Italian silver coins were exported to the other member countries where they were legal tender. Obviously, this enabled the Italian government to finance part of her deficits with seigniorage, the costs of which were shared between all four countries.

In response to the problems facing the union, a conference by the members in 1874 decided to maintain the bimetallic standard but restrict the minting of silver 5-franc coins. In 1878 the members agreed to cease issuing 5-franc silver coins although those already in circulation were to remain legal tender. This arrangement established the 'limping gold standard'. In the discussions preceding the decision of 1874, both Belgium and Switzerland were originally in favour of terminating the union and the Belgian delegates argued for adoption of a gold standard. France and Italy, however, were against both proposals, probably because the Banque de France as well as the Italian government feared huge costs of redeeming in gold all the 5-franc silver coins in circulation. The other three nations feared as well that a termination of the union might lead to Italy refusing to redeem the other countries' large holdings of Italian token coins. Instead, Italy had to agree to withdraw her token coins from international circulation for as long as she retained her inconvertible paper money.

As the relative price of gold continued to rise, the union in 1885 considered full adoption of the gold standard and thus withdrawing the 5-franc silver coins. The main problem was once again the cost of redeeming silver in circulation, since the intrinsic value of the silver was now far below its face value. In the end, this proved too great an obstacle to overcome and a new agreement was signed stipulating that any party leaving the union would have to exchange the others' holdings of its silver coins into gold.

The main cause of the break-up of the Latin Monetary Union was World War One. The sharp increase in military expenditures left the members with no choice but to issue paper money. The large quantities of paper money issued during the war remained in circulation after the end of the hostilities. As paper money was not recognised as legal means of payment in any other than the issuing country, the union no longer had any practical effect. During the war, silver coins were melted or exported. Remaining coins constituted a small share of the total money supply. Belgium was the first member to act accordingly, declaring in 1925 that she would leave the union at the start of 1927. The other countries followed and the Latin monetary union was dissolved.

The Scandinavian Monetary Union[26]

Prior to the formation of the Scandinavian monetary union in 1873, the three Scandinavian countries had a long history of similar units of account and exchange of notes and coins between them.[27] They were all on a silver standard. Indeed, in the years leading up to the 1870s, all of them used the riksdaler as the unit of account. One Norwegian specierigsdaler was roughly equal to two Danish rigsdaler which in turn was roughly equal to four Swedish riksdaler. As an effect of this, considerable parts of the coin circulation in each of the three countries consisted of coins minted in the other two. The difference in value separating these simple exchange rates from those based on

---

[26] This section is based on L. Jonung, 'Swedish Experience under the Classical Gold Standard 1873–1913', in M.D. Bordo and A. Schwartz (eds.), *The Classical Gold Standard in Retrospective*, Chicago and London: University of Chicago Press and National Bureau of Economic Research, 1984, pp. 361–99; and M. Bergman, S. Gerlach and L. Jonung, 'The Rise and Fall of the Scandinavian Currency Union 1873–1920', *European Economic Review*, Vol. 37, 1993, pp. 507–17.

[27] Finland was at the time a grand-duchy of Russia. Iceland was governed by Denmark. Norway was formally engaged in a political union with Sweden but enjoyed far-reaching political independence.

the currencies' values in silver was small enough for the Danish and Norwegian currencies that any profits which might have arisen from arbitrage were negligible. This was not the case for the Swedish currency. Its value exceeded 0.5 Danish or 0.25 Norwegian rigsdaler by an amount sufficiently large to produce an inflow into Sweden of Danish and Norwegian coins which was perceived as a nuisance there.[28]

This currency flow was, however, by no means the only reason (nor even an important one) for aiming at a unified coinage. In all of the Scandinavian countries, a lively debate regarding the most suitable specie standard – gold or silver – and regarding the merits of the decimal system for dividing the unit of account had created an intellectual climate in favour of converting the Nordic currencies into a common gold standard based on the decimal system.[29] The decimal system was favoured on the grounds of rationality. A currency based on the gold standard was deemed appropriate since Scandinavia's leading trading partners, the United Kingdom and Germany, were on the gold standard. In addition, the nationalistic sentiments running through Europe in the latter half of the 19th century took the form of 'Scandinavism' in Scandinavia – a social and political willingness to bring the Nordic countries closer together in many areas.

All of these factors – the disequilibrium in currency flows, the perceived superiority of the gold standard and the decimal system, and the political climate of the day – contributed to Sweden, Denmark and Norway creating a common currency union in 1873. Norway did not formally sign the agreement until 1875 but in practice her monetary standard was altered in 1873.[30]

The formation of the Scandinavian monetary union in 1873 replaced the old unit of account, the riksdaler, with a new one, the krona. The value of a Scandinavian krona was specified in terms of

---

[28] The law proposed in the Swedish Parliament in 1873 specifically mentioned the permanent costs emanating from the inflow of Danish and Norwegian silver coins.

[29] The issue was debated at three meetings of Scandinavian economists: at Gothenburg (1863), Stockholm (1865) and Copenhagen (1872).

[30] The reasons for Norway's initial refusal to join the monetary union are not entirely clear. In any case, Norway joined the union two years later and, in doing so, accepted all the terms of the agreement. She had already (1873) introduced all measures except the granting of legal tender status to Swedish and Danish coins.

gold and was to be equal in all three countries where the new gold coin was minted. Subsidiary coins were to be minted in silver and copper with a fineness of 80 per cent and without any restrictions on the amount of coins each country was allowed to mint. All coins were given legal tender status throughout the three Scandinavian countries. The state treasuries accepted unlimited amounts of coins irrespective of their country of origin. The only restrictions were a maximum amount stipulated for the settlement of private debts.

Because of the larger denominations of the gold coins compared to the denomination of bank notes, notes remained widely in use in Sweden. Inter-country circulation consisted of notes and subsidiary coins. This caused some dissatisfaction, since notes were not covered by the union agreement and thus did not always circulate at par. However, this shortcoming was eventually to be remedied.

The first enlargement of the Scandinavian monetary union occurred in 1885. The three central banks decided to establish inter-country drawing rights. Transactions between the central banks were made free of interest and other charges. It is unlikely that the central banks would have entered such an agreement if they felt that currency flows would create a permanent disadvantage. Consequently, the 1885 agreement indicates that no country sought to gain seigniorage benefits at the expense of the others. The smooth functioning of the union led Sweden and Norway to extend further the scope of the union in 1894 by accepting each others' notes at par without restrictions. The Danish central bank did not join the new agreement until 1901.[31]

No particular economic strains in the union seem to have appeared before World War One. The gold standard, by requiring convertibility into gold, ensured stability of the money supply. All three countries avoided issuing excessive amounts of subsidiary coins.[32] The money

---

[31] The comparatively less widespread note circulation in Denmark may have led the Danish central bank to treat the issue as less urgent. Notes represented 26 per cent of the circulation in Denmark, 41 per cent in Norway and 57 per cent in Sweden, according to I. Henriksen, N. Kærgård and C. Sörensen, 'Den skandinaviske möntunion', *Den jyske historiker*, Nos. 69–70, 1994, pp. 88–97.

[32] One event, however, suggests underlying political strains. In 1905, the Swedish central bank cancelled its participation in the 1885 agreement. A new renegotiated agreement quickly followed which allowed each central bank to charge the other banks when selling

supply in the member countries expanded in line with economic growth. Inflation rates and interest rates exhibited identical patterns in Scandinavia during the union. The effects of the union on intra-Scandinavian trade is an issue that needs more research. According to contemporary sources, border trade between the countries benefited from the union. However, intra-Scandinavian trade declined during the union period. The monetary union was not combined with a Scandinavian free trade area, however.

Like the Latin monetary union, the Scandinavian monetary union's collapse was induced by World War One. At the outbreak of war, Scandinavian notes were declared inconvertible into gold. At the same time, in order to prevent an outflow of gold, the export of gold was prohibited. The growth of the money supply thereby ceased to be tied to the supply of gold and the basis for the exchange of Scandinavian notes at par was eliminated. Monetary policy was more expansive in Denmark and Norway than in Sweden. Therefore, in 1915, the official exchange rates changed accordingly, with 1 Swedish krona buying more than 1 Danish or Norwegian krona.

Since the legal tender status of Scandinavian coins in all Scandinavian countries was still in force, Danish and Norwegian gold coins were exported to Sweden. The governments in Denmark and Norway often granted exemptions from the prohibition of gold exports. The Swedish central bank objected to the inflow of gold coins. Negotiations were opened in order to achieve the suspension of the legal tender arrangement. Neither Denmark nor Norway wished to terminate it, however, and the outcome in 1917 was instead a strict enforcement of the prohibition of gold exports.

At the end of the war, the three Scandinavian currencies were no longer traded at par. Gold coins could not circulate across borders because of the ban on gold exports. In virtually all respects the Scandinavian monetary union had been rendered ineffective by the war. The only remaining parts of the original agreement were the legal tender and equal value status and unrestricted minting and flow of subsidiary coins. Because the Swedish coins were more valuable than

---

drawing rights. This option was not used for five years, and then only by Norway and Denmark, suggesting that the action of the Swedish central bank in 1905 was motivated by a desire to make a gesture against Norway which had secured independence from Sweden that year.

Danish and Norwegian coins, subsidiary coins flowed into Sweden. To remedy this situation, a supplementary agreement was put in force in 1924 which stated that, without regard to the coinage treaty of 1873, each country could only issue new subsidiary coins that were legal tender in the issuing country, thus phasing out the common subsidiary coins in circulation. The union was effectively terminated by the 1924 decision.

Other Monetary Unions[33]

In the 19th century, currency boards developed as a common monetary arrangement in many colonies, in particular in British colonies. A typical currency board issued notes and coins at least fully backed by reserves denominated in the currency of the colonial power (see Table 1). Currency boards were a method of economising on the use of notes and coins of the colonial power.[34] A currency board represented a form of monetary union, more precisely an exchange rate union, between the colony and the home country.

Most colonies abolished their currency boards and established central banks of their own when they gained independence in the 1950s and 1960s. In a few cases the currency board system was maintained and made more sophisticated, for example, Hong Kong, Singapore, the East African Currency Area – emanating from British colonial rule but dissolved in 1977[35] – and the East Caribbean Currency Area consisting of seven small island nations.

Currency boards have experienced a renaissance in the 1990s having recently been adopted by Argentina, Estonia, Lithuania and Bulgaria. So far these experiments appear to have worked well in terms of establishing monetary stability and credibility relative to alternative monetary arrangements. However, it remains to see how well they will function in the long run.

---

[33] This section is based on B.J. Cohen, 'Beyond EMU: The Problem of Sustainability', *Economics and Politics*, Vol. 5, No. 2, 1993, pp. 187–203, and R.F. Graboyes, 'The EMU: Forerunners and Durability', *Federal Reserve Bank of Richmond Economic Review*, Vol. 16, July–August 1990, pp. 8–17.

[34] For a description of the workings and history of currency boards, see S. Hanke, L. Jonung and K. Schuler, *Russian Currency and Finance: A Currency Board Approach to Reform*, London: Routledge, 1993; and A. Schwartz, *Do Currency Boards Have a Future?* Occasional Paper No. 88, London: Institute of Economic Affairs, 1992.

[35] B.J. Cohen, *op. cit.*; and S. Hanke, L. Jonung and K. Schuler, *op. cit.*, Appendix C.

A number of monetary unions have been established in the 20th century. One example is the CFA Franc Zone, formed in 1959 by former French colonies in west and central Africa and still in operation today, which has much in common with a currency board agreement.[36] The zone is in practice two monetary unions covered by the same arrangement, with each union having its own monetary authority. Each union uses a unit of account called the CFA franc which in 1948 was set equal to 1/50 of a French franc.[37] The CFA francs are legal tender within their respective monetary unions and are convertible into French francs. France's influence over monetary policy in the region is substantial. The CFA Franc Zone has provided lower inflation rates than neighbouring African countries, primarily by limiting credit to national governments.

The East Caribbean Currency Area provides an example of a multinational monetary union with a single monetary authority. The East Caribbean Currency Area comprises seven small countries in the Caribbean Ocean that were previously British colonies.[38] Under British rule, monetary matters were controlled by the British Caribbean Currency Board, which has since evolved into the East Caribbean Central Bank. It is the sole issuer of a single currency for the union, the Caribbean dollar, which is legal tender in the seven member states. The seven member countries also cooperate in other matters, for instance through the East Caribbean Common Market. Again, the union is still in operation.

Some unions deal with the case of a very small country adopting the monetary system of a large country, most commonly a close neighbour, for example Luxembourg-Belgium, Andorra-France, Monaco-France, the Vatican City-Italy, San Marino-Italy and Liechtenstein-Switzerland. In each of these cases, monetary authority is exercised entirely by the larger country.

---

[36] More specifically, the members are Benin, Burkina Faso, Cameroon, Central African Republic, Chad, Congo, Equatorial Guinea, Gabon, Ivory Coast, Mali, Niger, Senegal and Togo.

[37] In 1994, though, the CFA franc was devalued by 50 per cent.

[38] The members are Anguilla, Antigua and Barbuda, Dominica, Grenada, St Kitts-Nevis, St Lucia and St Vincent and the Grenadines.

There are a few cases of a small country unilaterally adopting the monetary system of a country far away. Examples include Liberia where the Liberian dollar was fixed to the US dollar at a one-to-one rate and US bank notes were made legal tender in Liberia in 1944; likewise Panama, which in 1904 (one year after the country was formed) fixed the exchange rate of the domestic currency, the balboa, to the US dollar and made the US dollar legal tender.

The monetary union between Ireland and the United Kingdom formed after Irish Home Rule in 1922 represented a currency board institution.[39] Sterling was used in Ireland from 1826 when the Irish and British pounds were amalgamated. This arrangement was initially prolonged in 1922. With Britain as the largest trading partner of Ireland, the Irish government by taking no action to change the monetary system indicated that the advantages of maintaining close monetary links to Britain outweighed the advantages of monetary sovereignty. In 1928, a new Currency Commission began issuing a new currency, the Irish pound, which was explicitly linked to sterling. It had to be backed by gold or sterling assets one-to-one and sterling remained legal tender. The union was not ended until 1979 when Ireland decided to join the newly formed EMS, a step influenced by pro-Europe sentiments as well as by a desire to decouple from a weak sterling.

Why are Monetary Unions Created and Dissolved?

This account of the establishment of monetary unions points to some central causes of why unions are created. *First*, the most important reason is the existence of political unity. Once such unity is at hand, the creation of a monetary union eventually follows, and through history nation-states – with the exception of very small states like Monaco, Andorra and Luxembourg – have chosen to be part of a unified monetary area but with a national currency unit of their own. *Second*, economic reasons, including gains from trade, access to wider markets, reduction in transaction costs in exchanging money and harmonisation of policies, have played an important rôle in the creation of monetary unions. *Third*, there are also other non-economic

---

[39] The section on the monetary union between Ireland and Britain is based on J. Bradley and K. Whelan, 'Irish Experience of Monetary Linkages with the United Kingdom and Developments since Joining the EMS', in R. Barrell (ed.), *Economic Convergence and Monetary Union in Europe*, London: Sage Publications, 1992, pp. 121–43.

factors encouraging union – besides political unity – such as a common history, a common language, culture and religion.

Monetary unions have also been destroyed. In the 20th century, several national monetary unions have been terminated: that of the Austro-Hungarian empire after World War One, and the German monetary union which split after the Second World War into two parts belonging to Western and Eastern Germany. The political dissolutions of the Soviet Union, Yugoslavia and Czechoslovakia in the 1990s also brought about monetary de-unification. Table 2 lists some monetary unions which have broken up in the 20th century.

The events illustrated by Table 2 raise the question: why are monetary unions dissolved? The answer points to the central rôle of political unity behind the rise and fall of monetary unions. When far-reaching political events cause the break-up of existing nation-states into smaller territories, monetary de-unification follows as a corollary. The break-up and transformation into new monetary areas may be accompanied by monetary turmoil and high inflation as was the case when two European empires were dissolved in the 20th century – Austria-Hungary and the Soviet Union. The monetary union of Yugoslavia broke up in the face of a civil war. By contrast, the dissolution of the monetary union of Czechoslovakia was a rather quiet affair. To sum up, the causes of the fall of monetary unions are mainly to be found in political developments.

Table 2: Dissolution of Some Monetary Unions in the 20th Century

Monetary union	Time of dissolution	Causes of dissolution
Austria	1919–27	Defeat at war, creation of several new nation-states
Soviet Union	1992–94	Dissolution of the political régime, creation of several new nation-states
Yugoslavia	1991–94	Political unrest, civil war, rise of new states
Czechoslovakia	1993	Political divergencies, rise of new states

PART 4

LESSONS FOR EMU FROM THE
HISTORY OF MONETARY UNIONS

THIS REVIEW OF THE HISTORY OF MONETARY UNIONS – one created at the end of the 18th century and the other four in the 19th century – invites a few conclusions that have a bearing on EMU. We distil six lessons from the historical record.

First, the creation of national monetary unions was closely associated with the establishment of independent nation-states. In the United States, Italy and Germany monetary unification followed political unification. The existence of a nation-state was thus a prerequisite for monetary unification.

What are the implications of this observation for EMU? The EMU project appears to be unique in the history of monetary unions. We have found no clear and unambiguous historical precedents for EMU – where a group of monetary and politically independent countries have surrendered their national currencies to form a common monetary union based on a new unit of account under the leadership of a common monetary authority, while still retaining political independence.

The closest historical parallels are the national monetary unions which evolved in the United States, Italy and Germany. These cases show that a complete monetary union, that is, the use of the same money as well as a common monetary policy across all jurisdictions, remains functional in the long run when combined with far-reaching political integration. A prerequisite is that the members of the currency union give up their monetary sovereignty, which is an essential part of political sovereignty. This suggests that successful monetary unification will most likely be associated with closer political cooperation and coordination among the members of EMU.

Second, the history of national monetary unions suggests that such unions are permanent institutions. Their durability is a consequence of the political process that created the nation-state. To the extent that the political unity is strong and stable, the national monetary union will remain.

What are the implications of this for EMU? Joining EMU should be regarded as a permanent step for any European country. It would most likely be a cumbersome process to reestablish monetary independence once it had been relinquished in exchange for an institution that will function like a national monetary union – and the organisation of EMU seems close to that of a national monetary union.

Third, national monetary unions collapse as a rule when the political union that constituted the foundation of the monetary union disintegrates. Political disintegration can be an extremely traumatic process, as witnessed by the break-up of several monetary unions in Europe in recent years. It could also be managed in a 'civilised' way, such as the division of the monetary union of Czechoslovakia into the Czech and Slovak monetary areas.

The dissolution of multinational monetary unions, on the other hand, turned out to be fairly expedient affairs as seen in the two cases examined here: the Latin monetary union and the Scandinavian monetary union dissolved because of an unexpected major exogenous shock (World War One). The war contributed to divergent monetary and fiscal policies among the member countries. The dissolution was easy to carry out, as each member country had retained a central bank of its own.

What does this say about a future break-up of EMU? The conclusions depend on the type of monetary union that EMU will most resemble: will it be a national monetary union or a multinational union? In the very near future, EMU will remain closer to a multinational union. In that case, we do not envisage traumatic developments if EMU were to break up. The process would actually be similar to the break-up of the Latin or Scandinavian monetary unions.

The initial cause of break-up could be a major exogenous shock, particularly one which affects the members of EMU asymmetrically, combined with a lack of political will on behalf of one or a group of member states to adjust to the common policy of EMU. Here, only our fantasy limits the list of possible events or processes that could start EMU's collapse.[40]

---

[40] For one account of potential causes of dissolution of EMU, see M. Feldstein, 'The Political Economy of the European Economic and Monetary Union: Political Sources of an Economic Liability', *Journal of Economic Perspectives*, Vol. 11, no. 4, Fall 1997, pp. 23–42.

Fourth, monetary unions of the past, national and multinational, are in an important respect different from the present process leading to the creation of a common European currency. Monetary unification in the 18th and 19th centuries was based on adherence to specie standards. Specie standards provided a nominal anchor tied to a physical commodity (the volume of specie). The more-or-less fixed ties between specie reserves and the outstanding money stock limited the scope for discretion in monetary policy.

It was comparatively easy to create national or multinational monetary currency unions, since the members of the ensuing union, regardless of whether they were different regions or different countries, already had their currencies tied to a metal such as silver or gold. The monetary system remained a specie standard after unification.

The three national monetary unions studied here – those of the US, Italy and Germany – were primarily arrangements to reduce seigniorage competition between states or regions, to standardise coinage and establish national units of account. The different monetary entities (member states) of the new nation-states turned over their monetary, and thus part of their political sovereignty to the new nation. Eventually they gave up the right of seigniorage – an important form of taxation at the time. A national monopoly of seigniorage was preferred to competition. Moreover, although it was not important at the time, they also gave up their ability to influence their regional (domestic) economies by monetary policy.

The establishment of national monetary unions in the past should thus be viewed primarily as a way of reducing transaction costs and uncertainty about exchange rates. The existence of many kinds of monies within a politically unified area was regarded as a hindrance to trade and commerce.

The two multinational unions examined (the Latin and the Scandinavian) were set up to standardise coinage between independent countries. They were both based on the international specie standard of the day and they represented a closer degree of monetary integration than mere adherence to the specie standard. Each member continued to maintain a domestic monetary authority which facilitated the break-up of the union once it was subjected to large disturbances.

The relevance for EMU today from these observations is that EU-countries that want to join EMU are on a fiat – not a specie – standard.

A nominal anchor has to be created by these countries through some form of common monetary and political agreement to pursue and to enforce a rule such as monetary or inflation targeting. European monetary unification in the near future will be based on a commonly accepted, politically decided commitment mechanism as opposed to the gold standard of yesterday which had gold convertibility as a common focal point and commitment mechanism. The statutes of the future ECB set out price stability as its 'principal objective'. It remains, however, to be seen how this goal will be achieved.

Under the gold standard régime, there was no dispute about the character of the anchor, the process leading to monetary unification or the gold standard itself once it was in place. Today the policy framework is quite different. There is considerable uncertainty on this account over how the future members of EMU will conduct monetary policy. However, cross-country differences in opinion will have to be reconciled via a political process forcing independent countries to follow common policies once they are members.

Cooperation and harmonisation of policies under the gold standard was episodic and not by design – in contrast to Bretton Woods, EMS and EMU. A precondition for the EMU to succeed and be stable in the future is that the individual members of the EMU display forever a similar commitment to their common goal as did the advanced nations to the gold standard rule more than a century ago. This is a major challenge facing EMU. It is unclear how well it will succeed in creating such a convergence in policy preferences in the future.

Fifth, the political economy of national monetary unions suggests that such arrangements are dominated by one or a few major economic powers in the centre, not by countries or members of the periphery. In the United States, within the Federal Reserve system established in 1914, the Federal Reserve Bank of New York plays by tradition the most important rôle, in Italy the BNR emerged eventually into the central bank, and in Germany the state Bank of Prussia was the major element in the new Reichsbank, set up in 1875.

The history of international exchange rate régimes suggests a similar pattern, with the centre having a strong influence on monetary policies: the United Kingdom was the hegemon of the classical gold standard, sometimes working in cooperation with France and Germany. The short-lived interwar gold standard was dominated by the actions of the United Kingdom, the US and France. Likewise, the United States played the key rôle in the Bretton Woods system, and the ERM arrangement that failed in 1992–93 was based on the policies of the Bundesbank.

This centre-periphery pattern has implications for the future working of EMU and more specifically for the relationship between the major and minor member countries. An obvious qualification to the loss of monetary sovereignty for a small or minor country joining EMU is that it will take part in framing policy within the future European central bank system. Judging from monetary history we should not, however, expect a peripheral country, and thus a minor voice, to have a major influence on the decision-making process.

The political economy of EMU will primarily be determined by the major powers among the members of the monetary union – and most of the members will not be major powers because of the relatively small size of their economies. Of course, small countries may enlarge their influence by forming coalitions within EMU, but coalition-forming is commonly a costly process.

Sixth, monetary history suggests that monetary unification is an evolutionary process. It is hardly possible to set up a detailed plan for the process in advance – and expect the plan to work. The founders of the Federal Reserve System in the US could not have foreseen the rocky path that it followed in the first 40 years before it became a truly effective central bank. We should not expect EMU in the future to be identical to the EMU project that is presently being designed. It will develop over time in ways that we cannot imagine today. European monetary history does not end with the formation of EMU.

Further Reading

M.D. Bordo and F. Kydland, 'The Gold Standard as a Rule: An Essay in Exploration', *Explorations in Economic History*, Vol. 32, 1995, pp. 423–64.

P. Garber and M. Spencer, 'The Dissolution of the Austro-Hungarian Empire: Lessons for Currency Reform', *Essays in International Finance*, No. 191, February 1994.

C.A.E. Goodhart, 'The Political Economy of Monetary Union', in P. Kenen (ed.), *Understanding Interdependence. The Macroeconomics of the Open Economy*, Princeton: Princeton University Press, 1995, chapter 12.

COMMENTARY

FEW 'LESSONS FROM HISTORY'
Sir Samuel Brittan
The Financial Times, London

ACCORDING TO THE PHILOSOPHER HEGEL, the only lesson of history is that men never learn anything from history.

Such generalisations aside, Michael Bordo and Lars Jonung give us a very specific reason why the history of so-called monetary unions is only a limited guide to the prospects for EMU, and the case for and against other countries joining it.

Their key statement is Point 4 of their summary where they remind us that the régimes in existence prior to the breakdown of Bretton Woods in the early 1970s were founded on a specie or metallic standard, while the régimes of today are based on a paper or fiat standard. Thus comparisons of EMU with the 19th century German or Latin Monetary Union do not compare like with like.

For the first two-thirds of the 19th century European countries were not all on a gold standard. The authors explain that some were on gold; some were on silver; some used both, and some were on a bimetallic standard which tried to maintain a fixed ratio between the two metals. Moreover, coins were not of 100 per cent purity. There were examples, cited in the paper, of rules stipulating that they must be, for example, at least 83 or 90 per cent pure. And there were also many attempts to limit the circulation of small denomination token coins.

The various monetary unions of the 19th century were not concerned with the price level or sustaining economic growth or employment. They were, as the paper makes clear, mainly concerned with the complications resulting from the circulation of numerous coins of widely varying denomination and purity and with the absence

41

of a single standard of value for denominating contracts. The efforts to get rid of these obstacles to trade resembled much more the Single Market, which the EU is trying to establish, than the Single Currency. The analogy is with today's efforts to simplify and remove border controls or move towards mutual recognition of quality standards, or attempts to make tax systems more transparent, than they are with the attempts to establish a single monetary policy.

The euro has already had a rôle in increasing the intensity of price comparisons between different countries and thus making markets more 'perfect'. Since January 1999 there has been greater publicity for anomalous price differentials – not only in cars – between the UK and other countries. In a sense, Britain has been a free rider on the 11 founding members of the euro. Journalists and consumer advocates no longer have to compare British prices with those in a multitude of other countries. Even if they do not yet look at euro equivalents, they can make comparisons in national currencies knowing that exchange rates are 'irrevocably fixed'.

My guess, however, is that the single currency is less important in making markets more transparent than technical developments such as the Internet and other manifestations of IT, which make it possible for an increasing band of sophisticated consumers to make international price comparisons at the touch of a button

An international monetary union, without any metallic backing, is a novel undertaking. Money before 1914 was thought of as consisting of intrinsically valuable commodities. Paper money, to the extent that it was trusted, was valued for its convertibility into precious metals. Countries did, of course, occasionally suspend convertibility and move on to inconvertible paper currencies which floated against other currencies. But these were regarded as emergency measures undertaken in times of war or the aftermath of war. The intention was always to resume convertibility into precious metals as soon as possible.

History is therefore not a great deal of help in deciding whether a paper-based euro needs a common political authority. There is no escape from relying on general principles in assessing the prospects for EMU.

If one leans on the evidence to try to make a historical comparison, EMU emerges as a hybrid. It is like what the authors call a 'multinational union', in that it is being constructed without an overriding political authority. But it is like a national monetary union in that there is a single central bank – the ECB – which runs the currency.

The most relevant comparison is not with any of the past 'multi-national monetary unions' but with the international gold standard itself in the four decades up to 1914. This stretched well beyond Europe and covered, for instance, the United States. There had to be more-or-less a single monetary policy, as countries could not depart very far from prevailing international interest rates without provoking a run on their gold reserves. The nature of that common monetary policy was determined by the balance between the accidents of new gold discoveries and the efforts of official and private financial institutions to economise on gold stocks by all manner of devices ranging from convertible paper money to a proliferating array of credit instruments.

More recent historical comparisons are sometimes made. The chief examples are the harm done by the attempts to maintain unsustainable parities in the latter days of Bretton Woods or still more recent attempts by the IMF to maintain the parities of emerging countries before the Asian and Russian crises. Eurosceptics also often point to the conflict between the needs of internal monetary policy and exchange rate objectives when Britain was trying to shadow the D-Mark in the late 1980s or during the brief, sad membership of the ERM in 1990–92 from which the British establishment has not yet recovered. But this is still not comparing like with like. There is all the difference in the world between an *ad hoc* exchange rate peg – which even the rule-book says can in the last resort be changed – and the introduction of a new currency run by its own institution. In 1992 the markets rightly perceived a contrast between the needs of the UK for lower interest rates for anti-recession policy and the stance of the Bundesbank which, as a result of the inflationary forces following German unification, was reluctant to bring its own rates down. The worse the recession became, the more distrustful was the market of Britain's continuing membership until the whole structure collapsed.

With a single currency and a single central bank such a one-way speculative option could not occur. There would still be a problem if a country's domestic needs were for stimulus and the euro consensus were for restraint. But the situation would be ameliorated to the extent that there would be no sterling to speculate against.

A test of an opposite kind is emerging in the case of Ireland, which has economic institutions much more like those of the UK than of continental Europe and which conducts a large part of its trade with Britain. It has been experiencing a remarkable boom, which is tending to overheat the domestic economy. Left alone, the Irish financial authorities would undoubtedly have raised interest rates several times but, to conform to the single monetary policy, they have had to be reduced instead.

Pessimists say that the overheating will lead to an uncompetitive Irish cost level and subsequently to a severe recession. But there is another way of looking at matters. Existing federations, such as the US or Canada, often experience different rates of recorded price increase in different areas. Might not an overheated Irish economy be more like a California land boom or a Texas oil boom than like Britain in the run-up to a typical sterling crisis?

So long as productivity in Ireland is increasing faster than in the main part of the euro group, Ireland can afford faster pay increases even in the international trading sector of its economy. Price increases in the more protected sectors, such as real estate or traditional crafts, will not be tethered in the same way to the European price level and may go higher. But the kind of inflation psychosis in which people project an acceleration of inflation into the future cannot take place so long as there is confidence in Irish membership of EMU – which there is likely to be, in view of the country's political commitment.

Of course, there are big differences between Ireland and the UK. Ireland is a much smaller economy and has benefited proportionately much more both from inward US investment and from EU regional funds. Far more important: there is a pool of overseas Irish labour ready to come back when the labour market tightens – an anti-inflationary valve which does not exist in the UK. (Of course it could if we had a more liberal immigration policy.) Nevertheless, if I wanted a clue to how the UK might fare inside EMU, I would look at the Irish experience as it develops rather than at any of the 'monetary unions' of the 19th century.

The most important forward-looking remark in the paper by Bordo and Jonung is that the development of EMU is likely to be very different from what the framers had in mind or anything envisaged today. It is, for instance, often assumed that EMU will pave the way for a European political union, which will itself be a hegemony dominated by Germany – something like the system which the Kaiser's Reich might have established, if Britain had stayed out of World War I. The main ground for such an assertion is that Germany is by far the largest single member of the EU judged by either population or GDP. A supporting reason is the central position of the country, should the EU be enlarged to the east.

But I doubt if sheer size is all that matters. Even in those terms the German-speaking countries (Germany plus Austria) account for hardly a third of EU population and GDP. In terms of normal electoral arithmetic, they have a plurality but not an absolute majority. The actual political arithmetic of the ECB is even further biased against Germany. It has only two representatives on the 17-member Governing Council – or four if Austria and the Netherlands are taken as natural allies (the heads of the national central banks, plus one German member of the Executive Board). A tell-tale sign of underlying German insecurity is the fight it had to put up in the summer of 1999 to try to ensure that German should be used as one of the top official languages of the EU, along with French and English.

During the course of the negotiations to set up EMU, the fear was frequently expressed – not least in Germany – that German economic stability would suffer from being pulled down by the traditionally weaker Mediterranean and peripheral economies. The real surprise has been that the most successful economies so far have been these peripheral ones – above all Ireland, Spain and Finland. The one upward alignment that took place in 1998 in the run-up to the establishment of the euro was that of the Irish punt. The countries which have had the greatest difficulty in returning to normal growth and improving employment have been Italy, Germany and France. And if one allows for the dynamism of the unofficial Italian economy imperfectly recorded in the statistics, Germany and France alone may lead the rank of invalids in the economic sphere.

There are indeed problems ahead for the EU. But they lie neither in the absence of political union, nor in an excessive impetus in that direction, but rather from the ossified economic systems of these core states. European unemployment is not due to the supposedly hard line policy of the ECB – which maintains nominal and real interest rates below those of the US or Britain. It reflects, rather, excessively high and excessively rigid pay costs.[41]

In a static democratic environment, maintaining existing jobs and financing a margin of non-employed workers through the tax and

---

[41] I use this unsatisfactory expression because it is not so much pay itself, but the overhead costs of employing labour – social security contributions plus a great many restrictions on hiring and firing – which are the problem. But the formulation 'labour costs' is not satisfactory either. It is possible to hold down labour costs – as some German corporations are trying to do – by substituting capital for labour or by diverting investments towards the emerging countries. None of this helps with domestic employment.

social security system would be a legitimate option for rich countries. But it will not be satisfactory in European countries faced in the coming century with an ageing population and a looming deficit in national pension systems. If I can be allowed to indulge in a guess about what future historians might condemn, it would be the lack of attention being paid to the criminal absurdity of some European countries in trying to lower artificially retirement ages and shorten working hours and thus reduce further the production base available to finance the social security burden.

Neither a 'Europe of Nations' nor a federal Europe will make too much difference to the way these problems are tackled or not tackled – still less, the existence of the single currency. It is astonishing that so many supposedly hard money, anti-inflationary British economists and politicians should make so much of the absence of the devaluation option. John Stuart Mill once said that money was much less important than most people thought. This applies with knobs on to a single currency.

Many of the intrusions into the freedom of the British government to conduct its own policy, which are so resented by Eurosceptics, have nothing to do with the single currency. The attempts to enforce a minimum withholding tax on interest income – whether wise or unwise – arise from the Single Market programme. So do some of the regulations about product standards and quality. Restrictions on working hours or legislation on labour conditions arise from neither. In spirit they emanate from the Social Charter. But in legal terms they arise from a stretching of the interpretation of Health and Safety directives.

Those who think that a single currency involves uniform tax rates should look at the widely varying rates of tax in force in the different states of the USA. So should overzealous members of the Commission in Brussels. The one legitimate area of disagreement is whether a single currency involves, not a single tax policy, but a single fiscal policy. By this I mean a uniform attitude towards budget surpluses and deficits.

There is an unholy alliance between 'doves' and 'hawks' on this issue. The hawks around the central banks are all too ready to blame lax fiscal policies for any future difficulties in maintaining price stability; and the doves are all too ready to bemoan the restrictions – exaggerated in most discussions – placed on anti-recession policies by the Growth and Stability Pact. Those of us who believe that serious recessions and inflations have monetary roots – or at least are most amenable to monetary treatment – will be less impressed by either camp.

COMMENTARY

THE EURO AND HISTORY LESSONS

David Currie

London Business School

BORDO AND JONUNG PROVIDE US WITH AN INTERESTING HISTORICAL PERSPECTIVE ON THE EURO AND EMU. Although, as their bibliography makes clear, many scholars have examined the historical record on the creation and dissolution of monetary unions in the past, this record deserves to be better known. Their own foray into this field is therefore welcome. They note that there have been no examples of enduring monetary unions that are not accompanied by political union. They carefully do not conclude that EMU will fail unless Europe moves to a full political union, though some readers of their paper may well interpret their analysis in this way. But they do conclude that 'a precondition for the EMU to succeed and be stable in the future is that the individual members of the EMU display forever a similar commitment to their common goal as did the advanced nations to the gold standard more than a century ago' (p. 38).

British Eurosceptics will seize on this historical record to argue against monetary union. It is true that the only monetary unions that have endured in the past are those that have accompanied political union, so much so that we see these unions now as unified nation-states: Britain itself, where the English used military force to bring Scotland into the union; the United States; Switzerland; Italy; and Germany. The contrast is with the monetary unions that have not endured: the Latin and Scandinavian monetary unions, that of the Soviet Union, the *de facto* monetary union linking the British pound and the Irish punt, and the various unions associated with colonial empires (for example, the CFA Franc Zone, the East Caribbean Currency Area).

It is tempting to conclude from this historical record that monetary union can only work with a very high degree of political centralisation and integration. The loss of sovereignty that this implies is the principal objection of British Eurosceptics to British participation in EMU. And many of those who favour British entry to EMU, including myself, would also be sceptical if they thought that political centralisation in Europe was necessary to making the euro work.

There are two main reasons why I do not accept the lesson that some will wish to draw from the historical record that monetary union requires a high degree of political centralisation for its success.

First, it is important to note that the reasons why monetary unions have failed in the past have little relevance for the EU. They failed for essentially two reasons. Either the monetary union tolerated multiple central banks with the authority to print money, leading for obvious reasons to monetary chaos; or the grouping of countries drifted apart for broader political reasons, such as war, that had little to do with monetary union.

But these causes have little relevance to the EU today. The ECB has very clear and undivided authority over monetary policy. This means that the problem of multiple and conflicting monetary authorities creating monetary chaos through excessive monetary creation simply will not arise. The architects of EMU have been very careful to draft a set of rules that avoids the danger of a divided monetary authority, and to ensure participants sign up to these rules.

The second cause of break-up is the drifting apart for broader political reasons, notably the growing political tensions in the lead-up to the First World War. It is not impossible to envisage circumstances in which the broad coalition of countries forming the EU might split apart,[42] but this prospect is somewhat remote. The degree of mutual self-interest in the open trading arrangement that the EU represents is so great that it is in the interests of all to sustain it, and to ensure the conditions for its sustainability. The degree of interdependence between the members of EMU is certainly much greater than that between the members of the earlier monetary unions that have disappeared, whether measured through trade, capital market integration or cross-border FDI linkages. As a consequence, the costs

---

[42] See, for example, the scenarios set out in David Currie, *Will the Euro Work?*, Economist Intelligence Unit, 1998.

of splitting apart are very much greater, and the prospects of this happening correspondingly more remote.

This argument should not be overstated: European history in this century and the recent sorry record of wars on the doorstep of the current EU do not allow one to rule out altogether the possibility of hostilities in the future that would lead to the break-up of the EU. But the historical record shows that, as with the Latin and Scandinavian Monetary Unions, the causes of such a break-up are likely to be broader political developments that have rather little to do with monetary union itself.

The second point is that what the Eurosceptic argument based on history ignores is the unique nature of the coalition of nation-states that makes up the EU. Earlier federations involving monetary unions coalesced at a time when the nation-state and its powers were undeveloped. This left open the possibility that these powers would develop at the federal, central level, and this is what happened in all cases, though to differing degrees. But the EU is a coalition of already-developed states. This makes it less easy for the EU to develop by centralising power in a major way, for that would imply nation-states giving up major powers. The EU has therefore relied much less on central federal powers, and much more on forms of cooperation between the European states buttressed by a framework of law.

This distinction may sound a subtle one, but it is important. To give a specific example, earlier federations have evolved a system of fiscal federalism, whereby taxes and transfers are shared and redistributed across the constituent states, and many point to the necessity of Europe developing a similar system if monetary union is to work. But a more careful analysis suggests that there is no economic function that such a system would achieve that cannot be achieved by appropriate coordination of the existing national fiscal systems.[43]

The euro does not need federation in the usual sense of the word. What is being created in Europe is a quasi-federation of nation-states, which is not the same thing as a quasi-federated state. Europe is developing a new political form, based on cooperation between nation-states where it is in their joint interests, where it is in their mutual self-interest. The difference is reflected in the fact that the true focus of decision-making in Europe, the real European Parliament, is not

---

[43] For further discussion of this point, see David Currie, *Does the Euro Herald Economic Government?*, Centre for European Reform, 1999.

the assembly that goes under that name but rather the Council of Ministers.[44]

Europe is clearly in a state of evolution. It is possible in time that some countries in Europe will wish to put in place a tighter system of European federation that goes beyond government cooperation bound by legal undertakings enforceable by the European Court. Some might wish to go further and embark on the type of integration that Germany, Italy and Switzerland underwent in the last century, when different countries came together to coalesce into what we now regard as nation-states. And it may be that the EU will need to adapt to enable this wish to be realised. But a European federation that embraces all the current and prospective members of the EU will be unworkable, so such adaptation will have to happen in a way that respects the interests of those countries and peoples that do not want to go down that road.

It is more likely, however, that the EU is evolving a new governance structure, between the national federation and loose forms of international agreement based on cooperation between independent nation-states. The greater enforcement powers of the European Court allow deeper, enforceable cooperation than is feasible at the international level, without the panoply of powers entailed in full federation or European government. The euro both embodies this deeper cooperation and greatly expands the scope for it. This process will require the problem of the democratic deficit in Europe to be addressed, if European cooperation is to have the necessary political legitimacy. But that can be achieved without, and indeed is helped by the absence of, a high degree of centralisation in Europe.

As Bordo and Jonung note, 'monetary unification is an evolutionary process'. But given the different starting-point of the EU, with developed state powers at the national level, it is unlikely that this evolution will mirror that of earlier historical examples of monetary unification. In particular, the euro can and will work without European government and, by expanding the range of European cooperation, will strengthen the process of deep integration initiated by the Single

---

[44] An unsatisfactory aspect is the fact that the proceedings of the Council of Ministers are not on the public record, in contrast to democratic assemblies elsewhere.

Market programme. The result will be a healthier and stronger EU, to the benefit of all its members. For this reason, we should be aware of the lessons of history that Bordo and Jonung point to, but not blinkered by them.

COMMENTARY

IS EMU SUSTAINABLE WITHOUT POLITICAL UNION?

Walter Eltis

Exeter College, Oxford

THE PAPER BY MICHAEL BORDO AND LARS JONUNG OFFERS NO EXAMPLE OF A MONETARY UNION WHICH HAS SURVIVED WITHOUT POLITICAL UNION. It is important to understand why the successful monetary unions have either followed or been preceded by political union, while attempts to achieve monetary union without political union have failed. Their paper therefore contains searching questions for the 11 nations which embarked on the EMU project in January 1999, and for Britain if it decides to join after 2002.

There are three kinds of external shock to the individual members of a monetary union which can only be countered with the political agreement of all:

- asymmetric economic shocks which are damaging only to some,

- banking failures of the kind which have recently occurred in the US and Japan,

- military threats to vital interests.

The sustainability of EMU will depend on the ability of the 11 to find ways of cooperating to control the adverse effects of these if they arise. They may achieve this by merging their sovereignties to produce the new nation-state which Bordo's and Jonung's history identifies as the common factor in the monetary unions which survived.

Asymmetric Economic Shocks

EMU's lack of means to counter asymmetric shocks has been widely discussed. In a single national economy such as the US, regions which suffer disproportionately receive fiscal transfers which amount to around 50 per cent of marginal changes in wages and profits. These transfers arise automatically within a single nation. With uniform tax rates throughout a nation, the prosperous pay more in taxes than central government spends on them while the depressed receive more from central government than they pay in taxes. If there is a shock which damages a region, the prosperous will automatically make good much of the fall in tax revenues from the depressed. Any targeted actions which governments take in addition will transfer more than the 50 per cent of marginal incomes allocated to depressed regions as a matter of course.

Within the EU, fiscal transfers between member countries are restricted to a maximum of 1½ per cent of aggregate EU incomes, and most of this limited facility is precommitted to existing programmes such as agriculture. For money to be diverted from such programmes, the current beneficiaries would have to agree to transfer part of their incomes to the newly deserving victims of asymmetric shocks. Most present beneficiaries tenaciously hold on to their gains under the protection of their right to veto any change in financial arrangements within the EU.

The cost of future adverse shocks within Euroland will have to be met almost wholly by the countries which incur losses in GDP. Their budgets will deteriorate as growing unemployment and falling domestic incomes reduce their tax revenues. The Stability Pact to which EMU members subscribe will limit their fiscal deficits to a maximum of 3 per cent of GDP (most already have deficits of about 2 per cent), so those with deteriorating economies will be obliged to raise taxation to control their budgets. In the US and Japan, the world's largest economies, regions which benefit from favourable shocks fiscally cross-subsidise the hardest hit. Hence the adverse impact of asymmetric shocks will be far more severe in Euroland than in the world's large nation-states. With political union, Europe would acquire some uniform taxes which would automatically redistribute incomes from the newly prosperous to the newly depressed.

EU economies such as Britain and Sweden which are unconstrained by the Stability Pact can control the impact of any asymmetric shocks which are especially damaging to some of their industries. They can borrow if they believe that shocks will be temporary and devalue if a long-term improvement in the competitiveness of their remaining industries is required: Sweden adopted this solution in the early 1990s. Temporary deficit financing and devaluation, which are still available to Britain and Sweden, are both denied to the 11 members of Euroland.

European Banking Failures

In the 1990s the non-performing loans of Japanese banks reached 30 per cent of GDP (according to Japanese government sources). The Japanese authorities have now taken over banking debts amounting to more than 10 per cent of GDP to prevent systematic banking collapses. The knock-on effects of bank failures in the 1930s caused unemployment in the US, Germany and Austria to rise from the 10 to 15 per cent which is normally experienced in a severe depression to between 25 and 40 per cent. A post-Second World War recognition of the consequences of systematic banking failure led the US authorities to respond to the Thrift and Loans crisis of the 1980s by taking over bad debts amounting to about 9 per cent of GDP.

Europe would equally wish to avoid banking catastrophes such as these. Decisions just as bad may be buried within the accounts of some of Europe's banks. These may have been more prudently managed than their US and Japanese counterparts, but European bank officials have enjoyed the same incentives of large up-front fees when they persuaded any country or company to borrow, sometimes lavish kickbacks, and hasty departures to another bank or to a rich retirement when it emerged that borrowers could not service the loans they should never have received.

Such errors will be exposed, as they were in the US and Japan, when Europe's economies are hit by other shocks, like President Reagan's 14 per cent interest rates of the early 1980s, or the Japanese depression of the 1990s. In that event, the 3 per cent of GDP which an individual European country is allowed to add to its public debt will not suffice to rescue its banks. The political agreement of Euroland's 11 nations will be required if it emerges that any government needs to rescue banks which have erred on a scale comparable to their US and Japanese counterparts.

Military Threats to Vital Interests

Governments borrow massively during military conflict because its cost cannot be absorbed within current budgets. Europe hopes and expects that wars which go beyond a few weeks of distant bombing will never again occur. But European nations continue to have interests which they regard as vital. In the 1920s British governments based their defence planning on the assumption that there would be no significant war within 10 years. In the early 1930s they presciently recognised that this 10-year-rule no longer applied, and from that date long-term programmes to develop the modern military aircraft and the radar defences which came to be so desperately needed in 1940 began to be implemented.

In 2000 we are re-experiencing the optimism of the 1920s and no potentially expensive conflict is envisaged by any country. But the Stability Pact and the Maastricht Treaty would prevent the countries which subscribe to them from spending large additional sums if new hazards emerged. Acting individually, these countries will therefore be unable to conduct a foreign policy which involves a significant risk of future military operations.

In theory the independent sovereign nations of the EU could act together in a future international crisis. The various episodes in the disintegration of Yugoslavia have shown that, because any actions proposed by the EU can be vetoed by any single country, Europe can merely talk. Only NATO, with most decisions actually controlled by the US, has been able to act on behalf of the European majority. This emphasises the fact that, if a future military threat emerges, an effective European defence policy will be unachievable without some merging of sovereignties. In that event, the 11, constrained by the rules of the Maastricht Treaty and the Stability Pact, will rapidly discover that they need to move towards an effective way of acting together.

Britain, outside EMU, would be less constrained in what it could spend, but it would still need to cooperate closely with either Europe or the US to meet any significant new threat.

A Sustainable EMU Will Require Political Union

Bordo and Jonung show that it was largely circumstances associated with military conflict, and especially the First World War, which led to the formal breakdown of the previous monetary unions which were unaccompanied by political union.

The Latin Monetary Union lost its common coinage long before then. Its 'central coin' has been described as the 5-franc silver piece of uniform weight which circulated as French francs in France, Swiss francs in Switzerland, Belgian francs in Belgium and lira in Italy.

These were accepted as legal tender in each country. The price of silver fell in the 1870s and the face value of the Latin Union's 5-franc pieces soon exceeded the silver they contained. It was in the interests of countries outside the Union to return these coins to the Union and obtain their face value in gold, principally from France, its richest member. The nations in the Union competed to over-issue 5-franc silver coins in an effort to acquire purchasing power from each other, and Belgium even asked France to guarantee their gold value, a request which France naturally denied. The members of the Union had to agree to limit their issue, and after 1878 5-franc silver coins ceased to be minted in any country. The overvalued silver coins which remained continued to be honoured as legal tender, but gold and paper superseded the common silver currency which had been the Union's principal coinage. The legal breakdown of the Latin Monetary Union may have occurred after the First World War, but it had ceased to provide the majority of the money in use long before then. An equivalent failure in EMU would take the form of a preference for other currencies over the euro in much of Euroland.

There may be similar over-issues of euros within individual countries. In theory the printing of euros will be controlled by the ECB, through Euroland's 11 national central banks which act as its agents in each country. Because they will be responsible for the printing of euros which originate within their borders, forgery may become difficult to identify. How will a German shopkeeper or hotelier know whether the Italian-originating euros he accepts were printed on behalf of the Bank of Italy in Rome or in a technically sophisticated unofficial printing press in Palermo? It is much to be hoped that by 2002 when euro notes officially circulate, they will be printed like other national currencies in a single place under the immediate supervision of the ECB.

Many regard the circulation of illicit euros as a remote possibility, too dreadful to contemplate. The widely recognised threats to the sustainability of EMU if its members do not agree to merge their sovereignties into a single federal state (with the same means as the US to control the quality of its monetary circulation) are those with which this article has been concerned.

Those who run Europe are aware how difficult it may be to control asymmetric shocks and to agree on how to limit the impact of banking failures, if these arise. The future management of these and the ambition to achieve an effective European foreign and defence policy are among the considerations which have persuaded them that monetary union is a necessary initial step towards political union. Most British politicians who seek to join EMU expect to be able to achieve monetary union without political union, but that option will cease to exist if EMU evolves into the federal European state on which its sustainability is likely to depend.

If the federal option is not achieved, EMU could disintegrate if the difficulties which have been outlined above prove so damaging to any country that it faces irresistible pressure to resume its monetary and fiscal independence.

COMMENTARY

EMU AS A MONETARY ORDER

David Laidler

University of Western Ontario

AS BORDO AND JONUNG WISELY REMARK, MONETARY HISTORY DOES NOT END WITH THE FORMATION OF THE EMU. Nor does the evolution of the tools with which we analyse that history.

It is helpful to think about an arrangement such as EMU in terms of a concept sometimes labelled 'monetary order'; and some monetary orders seem better designed to survive than others. In particular, it appears from Bordo's and Jonung's fascinating historical survey that, when such an arrangement involves a common currency, it is most likely to survive if it is supported by a unified political order, which in the modern world has most often taken the form of a nation-state. Seen in historical perspective, EMU appears to be unique, not to mention risky, in that monetary unification is leading, rather than lagging behind, political unification. But of course national monetary orders can, and often have, run into troubles of their own, particularly, when based on fiat money.

Let me suggest that it is helpful to think of any monetary order as consisting of four components:

(1) a set of goals for the monetary authorities;

(2) institutional arrangements that permit those goals to be attained;

(3) private sector expectations consistent with them; and

(4) political arrangements that permit goals to be changed, institutions to be modified, and through which the monetary authorities can be held accountable for their performance.

When we put it like this, it is easy enough to see why monetary orders, whether national or supra-national, can fail. Policy goals (1) are sometimes multiple and can turn out to be incompatible, (2) and/or institutions can be badly configured for their achievement: consider the Federal Reserve Bank's dual commitment to maintaining the gold standard and preserving financial stability in the early 1930s and the paralysing division of responsibilities between Washington and New York, which left it reaching for both and achieving neither. Even clear and coherent policy goals (1) can fail to attain credibility (3), as with many an attempted stabilisation programme in recent Latin American history.

As to category (4), I would suggest that monetary history is moving us into new territory. The analysis of time inconsistency and the behaviour of interest groups has made us wary of treating the conduct of monetary policy as just another issue for democratic politics to cope with, but it is not everywhere that electorates will tolerate central bank independence on the Swiss or German models. In some places, for example New Zealand and Canada, where the monetary order is currently anchored on inflation targets, the involvement of politicians in setting them, as well as the efforts of the authorities to open up the execution of policy to constant public scrutiny, should be seen as striking alternative balances between the autonomy granted to the monetary authorities and the accountability demanded from them. Of course, transparency helps to ensure that the goals of policy are well understood and attract political support, hence strengthening them as an anchor for expectations.

It may well be that, in the past, the association between monetary and political union was based on money's rôle as a powerful symbol of national sovereignty. But even under the gold standard, it is hard to believe that questions of political control were totally out of the picture. The alacrity with which the system was suspended by country after country in 1914 is surely testimony to that. But nowadays, with the economic literacy of electorates on the increase, to say nothing of the information available to them, it is hard to believe that providing for political accountability is not more important than symbolising national sovereignty in the design of a successful monetary order.

This is an important distinction, because there is nothing unique about the nation-state as a vehicle for delivering political accountability. It just happens to have been the principal means of doing so for the last two centuries, but federal states are, after all, partly a response to the fact that it is helpful to delegate control of some matters to smaller entities. Nor is there a law of political organisation of which I am aware that says that there is something inherently wrong about delegating from the level of the nation-state upwards, providing that accountability to the electorate goes with it.

Viewed as a monetary order, EMU is very much an experiment. It has clear goals, to be sure. But whether the structure of the ESCB, not to mention the ambiguities of the Maastricht Treaty about just who is in charge of exchange rate policy, provide a structure that will permit these aims to be pursued single-mindedly, particularly when the monetary system comes under pressure, must remain to be seen. As a result, it is not yet clear just how firmly anchored expectations can be – surely one of the sources of the skittish behaviour of euro exchange rates in the last year. But above all, it must be asked whether, in enshrining the ECB's constitution in an international treaty that seems to provide a higher degree of policy autonomy than any central bank has ever enjoyed, the architects of EMU have not neglected to provide any means whereby those on whose behalf monetary policy is to be carried out can hold its executants accountable if they do not like the results.

Bordo and Jonung suggest that, because it is currently a union among nation-states, the dissolution of EMU, were it to occur, need not be traumatic. Perhaps not, but such a breakdown would be the first reversal of a federation-building exercise that started long before 1958, so we cannot count on that. Monetary history is a fascinating subject, but it would be better by far to pay attention now to EMU's flaws as a monetary order, so as to minimise the chances of the monetary experiment of its formation being followed by another involving its dissolution, however informative to historians the latter might turn out to be.

COMMENTARY

MUST POLITICAL UNION ACCOMPANY MONETARY UNION?

Anna J. Schwartz

National Bureau of Economic Research, New York

THE AUTHORS SUGGEST 'THAT SUCCESSFUL MONETARY UNIFICATION WILL MOST LIKELY BE ASSOCIATED WITH CLOSER POLITICAL COOPERATION AND COORDINATION AMONG THE MEMBERS OF EMU' (p. 35). They note, however, that the conduct of EMU monetary policy is uncertain and that 'cross-country differences in opinion will have to be reconciled via a political process forcing independent countries to follow common policies once they are members' (p. 38). They also comment that 'The political economy of EMU will primarily be determined by the major powers among the members of the monetary union – and most of the members will not be major powers due to the relatively small size of their economies. Of course, small countries may enlarge their influence by forming coalitions within EMU but coalition-forming is commonly a costly process.' (p. 39)

Those with an implicit belief that monetary union will succeed, despite acknowledged flaws in the design of the venture, look to political forces as the *deus ex machina* that will ensure success. The authors' comments reveal three underlying assumptions: political union greases the way for monetary union; the common welfare will animate political actions by the EMU members; and big and small members will settle amicably any differences that may arise among them. These assumptions imply that political deals can be struck that will appease members who do not see eye to eye with others. Each of the assumptions can be challenged.

- *A common monetary policy administered by the ECB with the objective of maintaining price stability will be inappropriate for some of the member countries.*
  EMU faces two divisive issues; one is cyclical, the other structural.

A common monetary policy must gloss over the fact that on any given date not all the members will be in the same phase of the business cycle. Those in a recessionary phase would be helped by expansionary monetary policy; those in a business upturn would not be. Countries that are disadvantaged by a common monetary policy may try to modify it in their favour. If they succeed, the price stability objective may be sacrificed. If they fail, why will political union reconcile them? The authors apparently believe that the countries will not insist on self-interested ends but compromise their positions in order to form coalitions. The coalitions will engage in horse-trading negotiations to accommodate conflicts in their desires. This scenario assumes that an underlying bedrock of goodwill exists among the members.

The structural problem relates to the mixture of high and low unemployment levels among the members. Countries with high unemployment need to reform their labour market rules. Political union will mean that reform measures will be decided not by national governments but by European political institutions. Countries that will be less competitive if others achieve reform will oppose it at the European level. Political union may worsen rather than improve the chances for reduction in structural unemployment. Moreover, some countries may argue in favour of monetary expansion rather than labour market reform as the way to reduce structural unemployment.

If there is dissension among the member countries about monetary policy, why should one believe that political union would overcome the problem? How? By bribing the recalcitrant ones?

- What is known about the political behaviour of EMU members suggests that *narrow national interests motivate them rather than the common welfare.* A unified Europe represents for France an opening to assert its equality with Germany, for Germany the opportunity to assume its rôle of the natural leader, for Italy and

Spain and the smaller countries the chance to be players in the EU institutions – the Council of Ministers, the European Commission and the European Parliament. Each is looking out for its own ends, not the common good. At the same time, there are special elements in the German-French relationship, with Germany yielding to French self-serving proposals that are not in Germany's best interests. Will Germany be willing forever to subordinate its concerns to placate the French?

• Small countries have more voting power within the European institutions than their size warrants. Those with higher economic growth rates than large countries within EMU will oppose efforts by the larger ones to pressure the ECB to compromise price stability in order to promote growth. Is this struggle for influence amenable to political deal-making? *Political union will exacerbate distributional conflicts* and increase political tensions between countries. Poorer countries will demand protection against external competition and additional transfers from richer members.

EMU Problems before Political Union

An underlying problem for EMU is that member countries have different preferences with respect to the level of the long-run inflation rate. One should not be misled by the embrace of the Maastricht convergence criteria for admission to EMU to conclude that there are no differences in preferences. These differences reflect the degree of pressure each member will face in financing budget deficits. Budget deficits may not present an immediate ground for concern, since there are many restrictions designed to make EU members avoid excessive deficits. The Stability Pact, in addition, obliges them to limit their budget deficits to 3 per cent of GDP and imposes penalties for failure to observe the limit. Budget deficits, however, loom as a real possibility over a longer horizon. The principal source of fiscal overruns over the long term is unfunded commitments by many governments for social security. Growth of social security expenditures to match growth of benefits for an ageing population will exceed social security tax receipts. One option for governments would be either to reduce benefits or raise taxes. Governments with a strong preference for noninflationary economic policy will choose this option. Some have embarked on this course. A second option for governments would be to run fiscal deficits with the expectation that the pressure on the federal level to bail them out would be irresistible. The central bank in these circumstances would accommodate inflation, but with increasing disaffection on the part of governments with a preference for non-inflationary monetary policy. Why political union would resolve this dilemma is not obvious. Dissatisfaction with this outcome would exacerbate tensions within the Union, possibly foreshadowing its collapse.

As the authors state, there is no precedent in monetary history for EMU. It was preceded by the creation of a Single Market. The operation of a barrier- and tariff-free single market did not require the next step, the adoption of a common currency. The adoption of a common currency in turn does not require the second step, the creation of political union. The second step, however, is merely the prelude to the ultimate step in the sequence, whereby the member states will give up political independence to a centralised authority.

The argument for political union as a condition for the success of monetary union appears to be that differences among countries in the legal, institutional and social framework will impair central bank independence. If members retained their diversity with respect to regulation, tax system and public services, why should that interfere with the central bank's commitment to maintain the stability of the euro? It is not institutional diversity among the participant governments that could undermine the single currency. The real threat is diversity in the economic situation of the governments and the consequent preferences each reflects with respect to monetary policy. Political union does not level this diversity.

Should Britain Join EMU?

The governments that joined EMU calculated that the benefits of joining would exceed the costs. Too little time has passed since exchange rates were irrevocably locked in for anyone to know whether each of them made an accurate calculation.

Britain, however, can judge by its experience when it pegged its exchange rate to the D-Mark in the ERM whether it would be a good bargain for it to join EMU.

The motivation for pegging the pound to the Mark was to import the Bundesbank's low-inflation credibility. The decision to peg ignored a crucial German development of the time.

To contain the inflation generated by government budget deficits in order to finance unification, the Bundesbank had adopted a highly restrictive policy. It made no allowance for the blow to the economies of its European partners that its interest rate hikes inflicted. High German interest rates and a weak US dollar drew capital inflows to Germany and the German real exchange rate appreciated. For the existing British nominal exchange rate arrangement to be plausible, Britain would have had to reduce its inflation rate below the German inflation rate or realign the pound. It was reluctant to deflate or to devalue, but in the end the market enforced devaluation.

From the second half of 1991 there was evidence of loss of competitiveness not only of Britain but also of other countries in the ERM, indicating to market participants that a realignment was predictable. A recession that began in the first quarter of 1992 worsened the situation of these countries. Traders had reason to believe that many currencies were incorrectly priced in foreign exchange markets. On 25 August the pound was quoted slightly above its ERM floor but did not recover, despite heavy intervention. To signal its commitment to defend the existing parity, on 3 September the Bank of England borrowed $14.5 billion equivalent of D-Marks from the market. The attack on the pound nevertheless continued. Because home mortgages in Britain bore floating rates, the authorities were constrained in their response. For the market this made the British commitment suspect. On 14 September the Bundesbank for the first time in five years lowered two key interest rates. Within a day sterling was at the bottom of its band. That day the Bank of England is thought to have lost $15 billion in reserves. On 16 September, the Bank of England raised the minimum lending rate from 10 to 12 per cent and announced a further increase to 15 per cent which was not put into effect. Sterling fell below its floor and that evening it was withdrawn from the ERM, temporarily at first and then indefinitely on 19 September. The next day the Bank restored its minimum lending rate to 10 per cent and lowered it to 9 per cent on 21 September.

There are two reasons for reciting Britain's experience in the ERM. One is that, while Britain could obtain from today's deep international capital markets whatever resources would be required to defend its parity, the price of doing so in the form of astronomical interest rates was ruinous to the health of the real economy. Since floating, interest rates have come down and Britain has enjoyed its best economic performance in recent decades. A second reason is that Britain has learned, along with other developed countries, to achieve noninflationary economic growth. It does not need to peg its interest rate to that of a low-inflation nominal anchor to get that result. It can do so by managing its own monetary policy. The ERM experience argues that the costs of giving up use of exchange rate policy outweigh the benefits.

Joining EMU is neither necessary nor desirable for Britain. Giving up its own monetary policy to be ruled by EU monetary policy will expose it to interest rate movements that are not appropriate to its economic situation and can plunge it into recession. It will be much better off if interest rate decisions are tailored to Britain's internal needs. Joining EMU is not desirable because it comes with a package of political commitments that centralise social and economic policies in Union institutions. Public choice theory teaches that the drive to centralise is in the interests of bureaucrats, politicians and judges, not the citizens of the countries in the Union who want to retain their distinctive ways of life.

British exporters who are eager for an affirmative vote for monetary union are starry-eyed because of the prospect of fixed prices for their goods and services. They are short-sighted. They will not escape the negative economic consequences of Britain's loss of monetary autonomy, should it make the mistake of joining the monetary union.

COMMENTARY

PUTTING THE CART BEFORE THE HORSE
Sir Alan Walters

AIG Trading, London

THE AUTHORS PRESENT A CONVINCING CASE THAT, HISTORICALLY, POLITICAL UNION WAS THE PRECURSOR OF MONETARY UNIONS. This throws into sharp focus the fact that, in EMU, monetary union is to precede some form of political union, the precise nature of which is at present quite unknown. There is no historical record of politically independent countries having surrendered their sovereignty to a supranational monetary authority. The central question arises: why has the EU chosen to take a leap into the dark here? Why did they put the monetary union cart before the political union horse?

I believe that the basic reason for putting monetary union first is that the architects of the EU believe that there was considerable electoral support for a monetary union, whereas there was little taste for a centralised political union among the peoples of Europe. The man in the street could be told tales of a European Commissioner starting with £100 at Heathrow and travelling to all the members of the EU exchanging his money into each domestic currency, finally touching down at Heathrow with about £60. In this widely travelled age, virtually all people could recall the hassle of changing currency, the massive spread of rates at airports and all the difficulties, in many countries, of exchange control. One money sounds a simple and most attractive solution. The objections to EMU – loss of sovereignty, one-size-fits-all and so on – seemed technical and unrelated to common experience. Most attractive of all, the euro was pedalled as the 'instrument of low inflation'.

The fathers of the EU from Monet to Delors dissembled but never disguised their ultimate goal of political union. Even the

European People's Party – the allies now of our own Conservative Party – declare in Article 2 of their statutes that the party's objectives include 'pursuing the process of the unification and federal integration of Europe with a view to creating the United States of Europe'. The people of Europe, as distinct from the clerisy and élites, were much more chary of such political integration.

Political union was thought to be a leap into the unknown with wide-ranging ramifications; in the Community there were very different views on the extent and nature of a political union. Germany always regarded the ultimate form of EU as some sort of federal state similar to the Federal Republic – the 'ever-closer union' of the treaties. France, in the shape of President de Gaulle, on the other hand, believed in a Community of nation-states – a concept which was to be defended by the exercise of the veto. As one would expect, over time the German view has become more acceptable with more and more 'qualified majority voting'. Even so, divisions on the form, extent and speed of political union continue to be the main source of disputes within the EU.

But the élites saw that, whatever the rows over political integration, there was the undoubted popularity of monetary union – at least up to recent years. The élites identified monetary union as the soft underbelly of political union. Thus Jacques Delors saw that there would be substantial approval for a monetary union which would, he thought, soon lead inevitably to a United States of Europe. I believe that Bordo and Jonung have shown that there must be considerable political union – and much centralisation of power – for a monetary union to flourish. But is there also a unique sequencing – first political union then monetary union? Will the EU fall flat on its face as it first fashions monetary union before political union? Bordo and Jonung's account does not endorse first political union then monetary union as the *only* sequence that can work. It is just that there is no record of a successful sequence of first monetary then political union. Was it never tried? It would be interesting to know. Bernard Connolly has pointed out that Luxembourg and Belgium had a monetary union and no political union. But presumably Bordo and Jonung would regard this as a pseudo currency board rather than a monetary union. The gold standard is often trotted out as an example of a long lasting monetary union, 1870 to 1931, which was not preceded by political integration. But as Bordo and Jonung (and Anna Schwartz) point out, there were frequent crises and revocations of unlimited convertibility; the currencies were not unified. Sovereign rights over their issue were still vested in the nation-states: no sovereignty was ceded to an institution like the ECB.

Bordo and Jonung do not explore in detail just why political union has preceded monetary union in successful unions. One may conjecture that the strains imposed by one currency – and I think we see that emerging in Italy, Ireland, even in Germany – give rise to political incentives to escape the constraints. With a United States of Europe, with a substantial budget to dampen the shocks to which all economies and regions are heir, they have more hostages in the federal system. The political union puts feet of concrete in the system, discouraging escape and enabling the Monetary Union to cling to its currency despite the costs.

This surely is why there has developed an urgency in the Commission's attempts further to integrate politically. For example, 'harmonisation' of taxes and regulatory systems has moved to the top of the agenda.

So, 'should Britain join the euro'? On all the evidence, including Bordo and Jonung's valuable paper, the answer is an unequivocal 'No'. If we decide to leave the EU, then the argument does not need to be made. For what it is worth, I would urge that Britain 'do a Hong Kong', declaring unilateral free trade in goods, services and money and dismantling the myriad of Euro-regulations – but that is another story. If we decide to stay in Europe, as both Labour and Conservative parties propose, then I still believe that 'no' is the best answer, although, at the same time, I would not rule it out forever. The main objection to joining is that the British economy is different from the continental economies in many respects. Our economy synchronises more with those of North America than with the continental countries. It is likely that, with one monetary policy, we would suffer perverse monetary policies. Furthermore, our general economic architecture is more like that of North America than the EU – and, one may say, none the worse for that. We are more open and less *dirigiste* than continental Europeans. And our economy flourishes on services rather than on manufactures.

That is the economic case for retaining sterling. Then there is a good political case for not joining the euro, which I leave to others to adumbrate. But I must finally mention the argument, much embellished recently, that Britain will not be allowed to continue its membership of the EU and remain outside monetary union. The legal position, however, is clear: we are signatories of the Treaty of Rome and subsequent treaties, none of which specifies that a member is required to be also a participant in monetary union. But such a legal restraint would not prevent the Euroland group bringing all sorts of pressure on Britain to join. I suspect that is the unfortunate scenario we shall see in the years ahead.